Utilize este código QR para se cadastrar de forma mais rápida:

Ou, se preferir, entre em:
www.richmond.com.br/ac/livroportal
e siga as instruções para ter acesso aos conteúdos exclusivos do

Portal e Livro Digital

CÓDIGO DE ACESSO:

A 00062 PEACE2E 3 48883

Faça apenas um cadastro. Ele será válido para:

Richmond

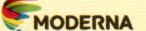

12120528 STUDENTS FOR PEACE 3 LA

Da semente ao livro,
sustentabilidade por todo o caminho

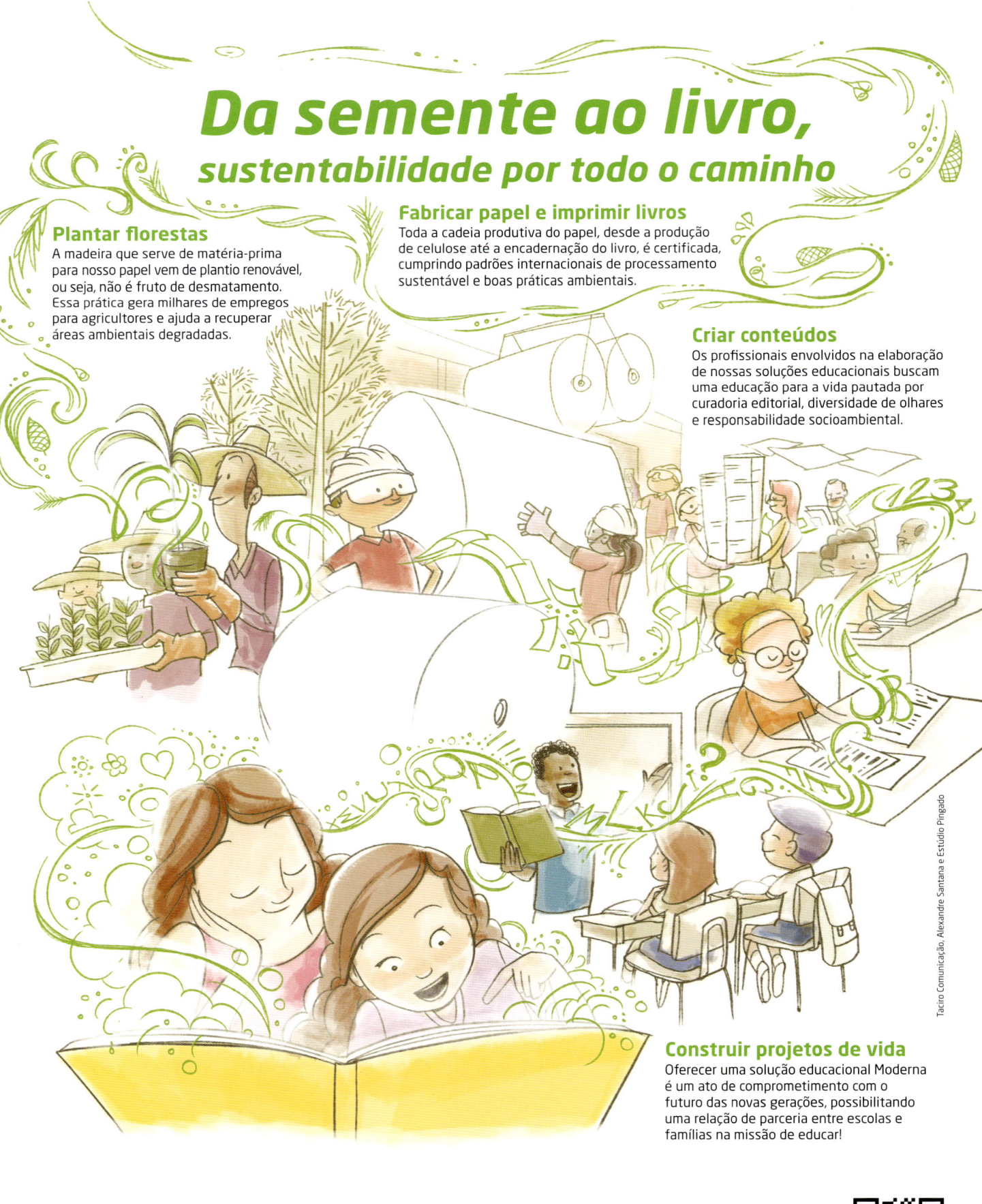

Plantar florestas
A madeira que serve de matéria-prima para nosso papel vem de plantio renovável, ou seja, não é fruto de desmatamento. Essa prática gera milhares de empregos para agricultores e ajuda a recuperar áreas ambientais degradadas.

Fabricar papel e imprimir livros
Toda a cadeia produtiva do papel, desde a produção de celulose até a encadernação do livro, é certificada, cumprindo padrões internacionais de processamento sustentável e boas práticas ambientais.

Criar conteúdos
Os profissionais envolvidos na elaboração de nossas soluções educacionais buscam uma educação para a vida pautada por curadoria editorial, diversidade de olhares e responsabilidade socioambiental.

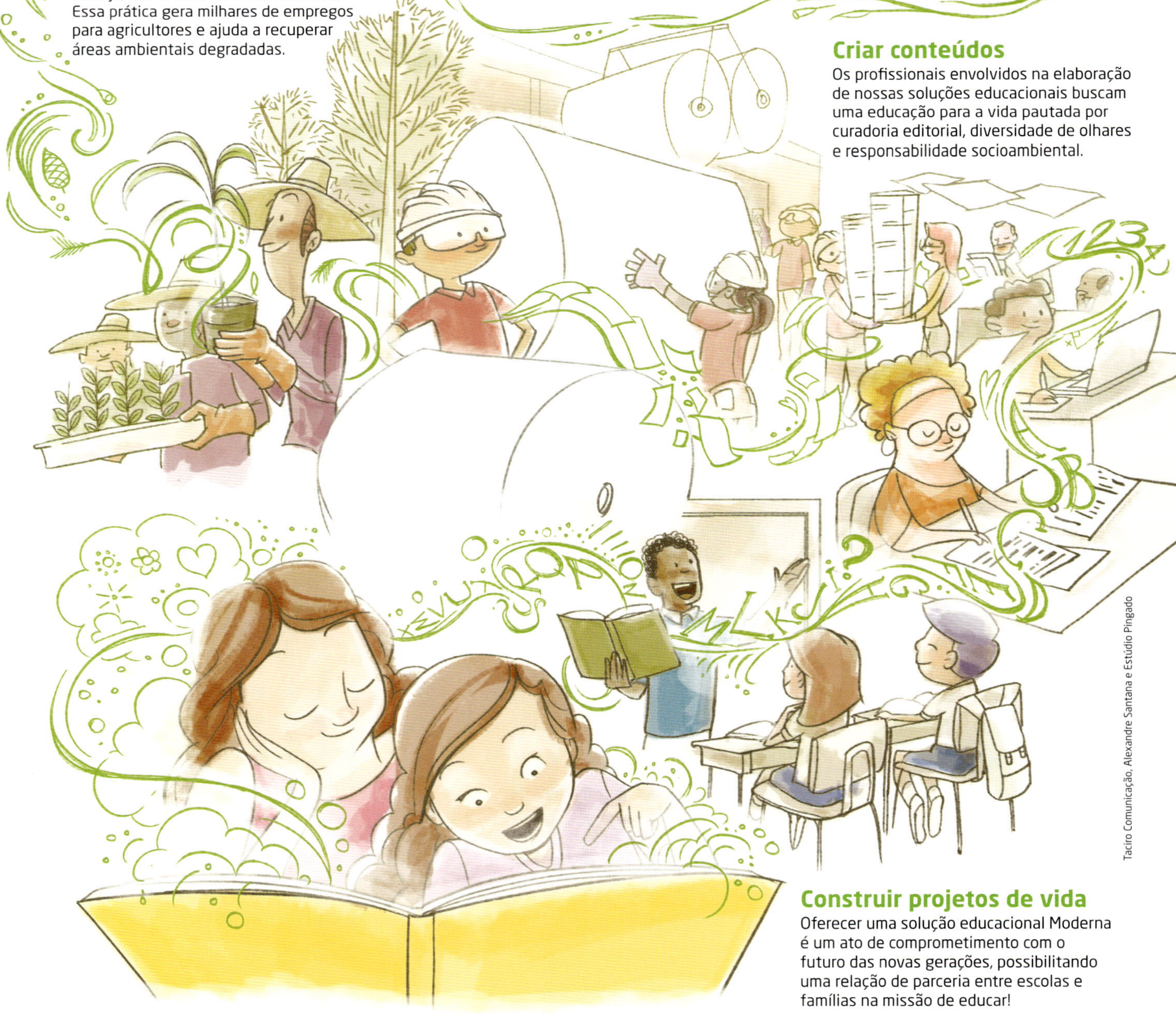

Taciro Comunicação, Alexandre Santana e Estúdio Pingado

Construir projetos de vida
Oferecer uma solução educacional Moderna é um ato de comprometimento com o futuro das novas gerações, possibilitando uma relação de parceria entre escolas e famílias na missão de educar!

MODERNA

Apoio: TWO SIDES www.twosides.org.br

Fotografe o Código QR e conheça melhor esse caminho.
Saiba mais em *moderna.com.br/sustentavel*

Students for

PEACE

Eduardo Amos
Renata Condi

3

Student's Book & Workbook

Richmond

Richmond

Direção editorial: Sandra Possas

Edição executiva de inglês: Izaura Valverde
Edição executiva de produção e multimídia: Adriana Pedro de Almeida

Coordenação de arte: Raquel Buim
Coordenação de revisão: Rafael Spigel

Edição de texto: Ludmila De Nardi, Nathália Horvath
Assistência editorial: Angela Cristina Costa Neves, Cíntia Afarelli Pereira, Leila Scatena
Elaboração de conteúdo: Ana Paula Reis, Beatriz Nosé, Christiane Araújo, Cristina Mayer, Doris Soares
Preparação de originais: Helaine Albuquerque, Roberta Moratto Risther
Revisão: Carolina Waideman, Flora Manzione, Gabriele Martin Cândido, Gislaine Caprioli Costa, Kandy Saraiva, Katia Gouveia Vitale, Márcio Martins, Maria Luisa Prandina Rodrigues, Marina de Andrade, Vivian Cristina de Souza

Projeto gráfico: Carol Duran
Edição de arte: Carol Duran
Diagramação: Anexo Produção Editorial
Capa: Carol Duran
Ilustração da capa: Jorge Pepelife
Criações: Anderson Sunakozawa, Carol Duran, Manuel Miramontes

***Website*:** Daniela Carrete, Frodo Almeida (*design*)
***Social Media*:** Ana Paula Campos, Priscila Oliveira Vieira (edição de conteúdo); Eloah Cristina (analista de projetos); Altair Sampaio, Frodo Almeida (*design*)
***Digital Hub*:** Ana Paula Campos, Priscila Oliveira Vieira (edição de conteúdo); Eloah Cristina (analista de projetos); Daniela Carrete (*design*)
***PEACE Builders*:** Ana Paula Campos (edição de conteúdo); Daniela Carrete (*design*)
***Digital Academy*:** Gabrielle Navarro, Thaís Teixeira Tardivo (edição de conteúdo); Daniel Favalli (coordenação de produção); Angela Urbinatti, Mônica M. Oldrine (*design*)
Novo Portal Educacional Richmond: Sheila Rizzi (edição)
Livro Digital Interativo: Gabrielle Navarro, Thaís Teixeira Tardivo (edição de conteúdo); Daniel Favalli (coordenação de produção); Angela Urbinatti (*design*)

Iconografia: Marcia Sato, Sara Alencar
Coordenação de *bureau*: Rubens M. Rodrigues
Tratamento de imagens: Fernando Bertolo, Joel Aparecido, Luiz Carlos Costa, Marina M. Buzzinaro
Pré-impressão: Alexandre Petreca, Everton L. de Oliveira, Márcio H. Kamoto, Vitória Sousa
Áudio: Maximal Studio

Impressão e acabamento: Coan Indústria Gráfica Ltda.
Lote: 284782 / 284783

Dados Internacionais de Catalogação na Publicação (CIP)
(Câmara Brasileira do Livro, SP, Brasil)

Amos, Eduardo
Students for peace / Eduardo Amos, Renata Condi. -- 2. ed. -- São Paulo : Moderna, 2019. -- (Students for peace)

Obra em 4 v. do 6º ao 9º ano.

1. Inglês (Ensino fundamental) I. Condi, Renata. II. Título. III. Série.

19-26387 CDD-372.652

Índices para catálogo sistemático:
1. Inglês : Ensino fundamental 372.652
Maria Paula C. Riyuzo - Bibliotecária - CRB-8/7639

ISBN 978-85-16-12052-8 (LA)
ISBN 978-85-16-12053-5 (LP)

RICHMOND
EDITORA MODERNA LTDA.
Rua Padre Adelino, 758 – Belenzinho
São Paulo – SP – Brasil – CEP 03303-904
www.richmond.com.br
2019

Impresso no Brasil

Créditos das fotos: Capa: RadomanDurkovic/iStockphoto; p. 6: Rawpixel/iStockphoto, AleksandarNakic/iStockphoto; p. 7: FG Trade/iStockphoto, gbh007/iStockphoto, monkeybusinessimages/iStockphoto; p. 8: Who is Danny/Shutterstock, metamorworks/iStockphoto; p. 9: agsandrew/iStockphoto, 3000ad/iStockphoto; p. 10: Brilliantist Studio/Shutterstock, Lisa-Blue/iStockphoto, yuoak/iStockphoto; p. 11: Anchiy/iStockphoto, pixelfit/iStockphoto; p. 12: polygraphus/iStockphoto; pijama61/iStockphoto; p. 14: Brian Niles/iStockphoto, gustavofrazao/iStockphoto, PeopleImages/iStockphoto, FG Trade/iStockphoto; p. 15: yacobchuk/iStockphoto, monsitj/iStockphoto, subjug/iStockphoto; p. 16: Pavel_Chag/iStockphoto, georgeclerk/iStockphoto, haryigit/iStockphoto, wildpixel/iStockphoto; p. 20: Steve Debenport/iStockphoto, skynesher/iStockphoto; p. 21: fstop123/iStockphoto, ferrantraite/iStockphoto, JAJMO/iStockphoto, FatCamera/iStockphoto; p. 22: GeorgePeters/iStockphoto; p. 24: palangsi/iStockphoto, VladimirFLoyd/iStockphoto, Lana Veshta/Shutterstock, metamorworks/iStockphoto, iStockphoto; p. 25: nycshooter/iStockphoto, damircudic/iStockphoto, nensuria/iStockphoto, kupicoo/iStockphoto; p. 26: ©1974 Peanuts Worldwide LLC. / Dist. by Andrews McMeel Syndication; p. 28: Wavebreakmedia/iStockphoto, MarkHatfield/iStockphoto, bodnarchuk/iStockphoto, hsyncoban/iStockphoto, Tero Vesalainen/iStockphoto, AzmanL/iStockphoto; p. 30: KidsHealth; p. 32: Wavebreakmedia/iStockphoto; p. 33: Floortje/iStockphoto, CreativeNature_nl/iStockphoto; p. 34: NataliaDeriabina/iStockphoto, Corbis Documentary/Getty Images, double_p/iStockphoto; p. 35: torukojin/iStockphoto, Tristan Fewings/Getty Images; p. 36: Ajay Verma/Reuters/Fotoarena; p. 39: Idealnabaraj/iStockphoto; p. 40: scyther5/iStockphoto; p. 41: deborahkr/iStockphoto, Ron_Thomas/iStockphoto, Greg WOOD/AFP, Derek Brumby/iStockphoto, Manuel Findeis/Shutterstock, Marcelo Alex/Shutterstock; p. 42: 270770/iStockphoto, pictorius/iStockphoto, Peter Voronov/Shutterstock, Bombaert/iStockphoto, RyanJLane/iStockphoto, pwrmc/Shutterstock; p. 44: Leremy/Shutterstock; p. 46: Willbrasil21/iStockphoto; The Courtauld Gallery, London; p. 47: Alexander Mazurkevich/Shutterstock, Birute/iStockphoto, ©Sebastião Salgado; p. 48: Dan Meshkov/iStockphoto; p. 49: ©Sebastião Salgado; p. 50: Frank & Ernest, Bob Thaves ©2001 Thaves / Dist. by Andrews McMeel Syndication, Frank & Ernest, Bob Thaves ©1998 Thaves / Dist. by Andrews McMeel Syndication, bbourdages/iStockphoto; p. 51: DutchScenery/iStockphoto; p. 52: Anahy Modeneis/iStockphoto, Cesar Diniz/Pulsar Imagens, Scott Barbour/Getty Images, Romulo Fialdini/Tempo Composto/Tarsila do Amaral Empreedimentos; p. 53: Musees Royaux des Beaux-Arts de Belgique, Brussels, ©Muniz, Vik / Licenciado por AUTVIS, Brasil, 2019, Nasjonalgalleriet, Oslo, Mark Langan; p. 54: The Museum of Modern Art MOMA, ©Wyeth, Andrew / Licenciado por AUTVIS, Brasil, 2019; p. 58: Renato Mangolin, emka74/Shutterstock, hamikus/iStockphoto; p. 59: ©Succession Pablo Picasso/AUTVIS, Brasil, 2019; p. 60: Hepworthfilm, Disney/Pixar; p. 61: PVR Pictures, ©UNICEF Moçambique/2011, NebojsaKuzmanovic/iStockphoto; p. 62: Lionsgate; p. 63 DMEPhotography/iStockphoto, FG Trade/iStockphoto, Capuski/iStockphoto, Igor Alecsander/iStockphoto, Pollyana Ventura/iStockphoto; p. 65: Corgi Childrens, Lionsgate, xavierarnau/iStockphoto, Yobro10/iStockphoto; p. 66: MK2 Productions; p. 67: lara_zanarini/iStockphoto, Geber86/iStockphoto, tilo/iStockphoto, MATJAZ SLANIC/iStockphoto, FredFroese/iStockphoto, PeopleImages/iStockphoto, MATJAZ SLANIC/iStockphoto, oleg66/iStockphoto, Razvan Ionut Dragomirescu/Shutterstock, Pobytov/iStockphoto; p. 68: jacoblund/iStockphoto; p. 70: asiseeit/iStockphoto; p. 72: Tashi-Delek/iStockphoto, Recorded Books; p. 73: urfinguss/iStockphoto, Martins Fontes, Luciano Joaquim/Shutterstock; p. 74: CreateSpace Independent Publishing, patrimonio designs ltd/Shutterstock; p. 75: Vectorios2016/iStockphoto, Giant Stock/Shutterstock; p. 78: Giant Stock/Shutterstock; p. 79: Pollyana Ventura/iStockphoto; p. 80: CreateSpace Independent Publishing, Townsend Press, Four Birds Education, IDW, HarperCollins, Bantam; p. 81: traveler1116/iStockphoto; p. 85: Suthichai Hantrakul/Shutterstock, Suthichai Hantrakul/Shutterstock; p. 86: Alex Ruhl/Shutterstock, Rawpixel/iStockphoto, mammuth/iStockphoto; p. 87: Matheus Obst/iStockphoto, Exclusive Lab/iStockphoto; Rawpixel.com/Shutterstock; p. 88: 20th Century Fox, HarperCollins, AF-studio/iStockphoto; p. 89: carduus/iStockphoto, YasnaTen/iStockphoto; p. 91: NEW LINE CINEMA/THE SAUL ZAENTZ COMPANY/WINGNUT FILMS/VINET, PIERRE/Album/Fotoarena; p. 93: 13_Phunkod/Shutterstock, Ridofranz/iStockphoto, AndreyPopov/iStockphoto, juststock/iStockphoto, PeopleImages/iStockphoto; p. 94: yayayoyo/iStockphoto, denisgorelkin/iStockphoto, Tigatelu/iStockphoto, denisgorelkin/iStockphoto, yayayoyo/iStockphoto, tanuha2001/Shutterstock, asliozber/Shutterstock, Julia Kuznetsova/Shutterstock; p. 95: tinnakorn/iStockphoto, tumdee/iStockphoto, chokkicx/iStockphoto, bodrumsurf/iStockphoto, Cartarium/iStockphoto; p. 96: DisobeyArt/iStockphoto; p. 98: Prykhodov/iStockphoto, monkeybusinessimages/iStockphoto; p. 99: Rawpixel.com/Shutterstock, vm/iStockphoto; p. 100: World Health Organization; p. 103: simonkr/iStockphoto, Wavebreakmedia/iStockphoto, Alexandre Tokitaka/Pulsar Imagens, TasfotoNL/iStockphoto, Brothers91/iStockphoto, hocus-focus/iStockphoto; p. 106: ALEAIMAGE/iStockphoto; p. 110: NatBasil/Shuttestock, Mojito_mak/Shutterstock, panuwat phimpha/Shutterstock; p. 113: fizkes/iStockphoto, DisobeyArt/Shutterstock, Igor Alecsander/iStockphoto, monkeybusinessimages/iStockphoto, stu99/iStockphoto, martin-dm/iStockphoto, 360b/Shutterstock, gradyreese/iStockphoto, Wavebreakmedia/iStockphoto, Tassii/iStockphoto, JohnnyGreig/iStockphoto, Rolf G Wackenberg/Shutterstock, m-imagephotography/iStockphoto, Juanmonino/iStockphoto, Sidekick/iStockphoto, PeopleImages/iStockphoto, HRAUN/iStockphoto, JohnnyGreig/iStockphoto; p. 115: kcline/iStockphoto, clubfoto/iStockphoto, damedeeso/iStockphoto, belchonock/iStockphoto, tmprtmpr/iStockphoto, DmitriMaruta/iStockphoto; p. 116: Imgorthand/iStockphoto, Mykyta Dolmatov/iStockphoto; p. 117: LPETTET/iStockphoto, Toa55/iStockphoto, rvika/iStockphoto; p. 119: John_Silver/Shutterstock, Andrey Shcherbukhin/Shutterstock, aljanabi/iStockphoto, Jeff Overs/BBC News & Current Affairs/Getty Images; p. 122: Edward Echwalu/©Walt Disney Pictures/Everett Collection/Fotoarena; p. 123: Scott Metzger/Cartoonstock; p. 124: keiichihiki/iStockphoto, WLDavies/iStockphoto; p. 125: DanieleGay/Shuttestock, Nomadsoul1/iStockphoto, mihailomilovanovic/iStockphoto, Pobytov/iStockphoto, Evgeny_D/iStockphoto, pepifoto/iStockphoto, lukacstamas00/iStockphoto; p. 127: artisteer/iStockphoto; p. 128: iStockphoto; p. 142: Cosmos Studio, Hachette, Disney/Pixar; p. 143: Video nas Aldeias, Scribner Book Company.

Dear student,

This is **Students for PEACE** – a set of materials designed not only to help you learn English, but also to make you think about, discuss and act upon important issues related to your life and your community. **Students for PEACE** is the result of many years of study and research.

When we first sat down to write this series, we felt that we had to go beyond the study of the English language because there was something the world needed desperately – peace. And it still needs it. So we decided to make peace education the core of this series and its goal. The ideas presented in **Students for PEACE** are based on the positive concept of peace as justice, tolerance and respect.

This series will certainly help you learn English, but we hope they will also help you understand and acknowledge human diversity and live with one another in harmony, facing the different challenges of the world around you.

As those famous song lyrics said, "All we are saying is give peace a chance!"

Have a nice year!

Editorial team

Scope & sequence

Welcome Chapter (p. 6)	Our history is a mixture of our personal stories			
	Goals	**Explore & Studio**	**Building blocks & Toolbox**	**Sync – Listening & Sync – Speaking**
1 In the future (p. 8)	• Reflect on different predictions for the future made both by scientists and laypeople. • Understand and produce an oral presentation with predictions about technological innovations for the future. • Understand and produce microblog texts about technological and scientific predictions for the future. • Understand and use adverbs to indicate (un)certainty in the future. • Understand and use the future simple to make predictions and express expectations in the future.	• Microblog post	• Adverbs to talk about the future • Future simple	• What does the future hold? • Predicting the future
2 Health (p. 20)	• Discuss physical, mental and emotional health, especially during adolescence. • Identify healthy habits. • Recognize and understand affixes (prefixes and suffixes) in word formation. • Understand and produce oral personal stories about health issues. • Understand and produce written personal stories. • Understand and use “some”, “any”, “many” and “much”. • Understand the concept of health.	• Personal story	• Affixes (prefixes and suffixes) • “Some”, “any”, “many”, “much”	• Talking about health issues • Personal story
Peace talk (p. 32)	The healing power of laughter			
3 Time to celebrate! (p. 34)	• Get to know and explore celebrations related to the English language as well as to other languages, recognizing the diversity among different cultures. • Make an oral presentation about traditional/folk songs. • Reflect on the importance of understanding the historical reasons behind celebrations. • Review the present simple in the affirmative, negative and interrogative forms. • Understand an oral presentation about the history of traditional Irish songs. • Understand and produce an informational text about celebrations. • Understand and use the names of the months. • Understand the use of ordinal numbers in dates.	• Informational text	• Months and ordinal numbers • Present simple (review)	• Traditional folk music • A brief history of some types of folk music
4 Art (p. 46)	• Describe and compare works of art. • Develop aesthetic fluency. • Recognize different kinds of art, especially visual ones. • Reflect on the role of art as an agent of change in society. • Understand and create an audio guide describing a work of art. • Understand and use the comparative form of adjectives. • Understand informational texts about art.	• Informational text about a work of art • Comparing art	• Kinds of art • Comparative adjectives	• Audio guides in museums • Creating an audio guide
Peace talk (p. 58)	Art for peace			

Unit	Goals	Explore & Studio	Building blocks & Toolbox	Sync – Listening & Sync – Speaking
5 Movie world (p. 60)	• Give an oral opinion about your favorite movie. • Participate in an oral discussion about movie preferences. • Reflect on the role of movies as a way to raise awareness about a cause. • Understand and use vocabulary related to movie genres. • Understand the main ideas of a movie synopsis and its reviews. • Understand the superlative form of the adjectives when giving opinions about movies. • Write a movie review.	• Movie synopsis and review • Movie review	• Movie genres • Superlative adjectives	• Teen talk • Discussion: favorite movies
6 From cover to cover (p. 72)	• Express preferences about reading. • Identify some of the main literary genres. • Make a summary of a literary piece for an oral presentation. • Read and explore excerpts from literary pieces. • Review the uses of the past simple and the past continuous. • Understand an oral summary of a literary piece. • Write a piece of short fiction (microfiction).	• A classic of literature • Microfiction	• Literary genres • Past simple x Past continuous (review)	• A novel summary • Summarizing a book
Peace talk (p. 84)	Safeguarding oral traditions			
7 Communication (p. 86)	• Discuss the meaning of some gestures and expressions in different cultures. • Identify different means of communication and think about their pros and cons. • Make predictions about the future of communication. • Recognize and use the future tense with "will" and "going to". • Recognize the characteristics of "notes" and "letters". • Write a letter telling someone about your future plans and dreams and asking about this person's plans and dreams.	• Notes and letters • Writing a letter about your dreams and plans	• Means of communication • "Will" x "going to"	• Gestures in different cultures • The future of communication
8 What's (in the) news? (p. 98)	• Reflect on the importance of critical thinking when reading news in the media. • Understand and produce a written piece of news. • Understand and produce an oral piece of news. • Understand the use of relative pronouns ("who", "which", "that", "whose") in subordinate clauses. • Understand the vocabulary used to talk about different media coverage.	• News story	• Words used in the news industry • Relative pronouns	• A TV news story • This is the news
Peace talk (p. 110)	E-safety issues			

Welcome to Students for PEACE!

Our history is a mixture of our personal stories

1 Read the spidergram and think of the answers to its items.

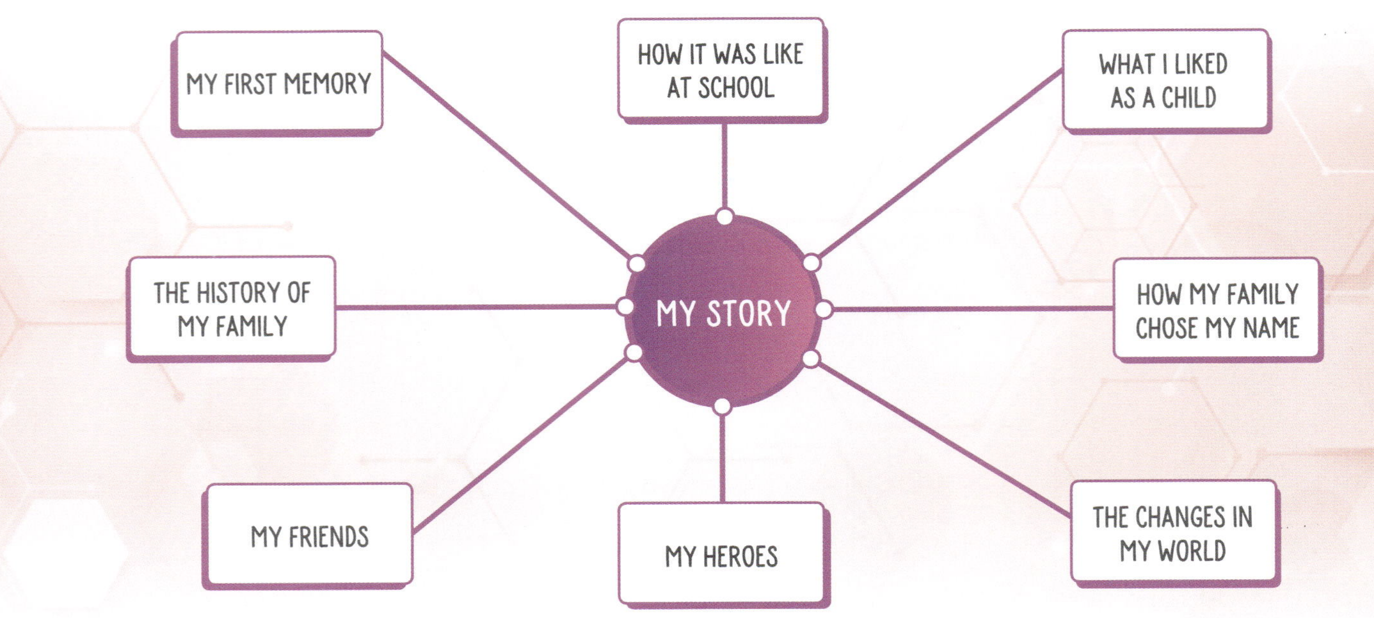

2 Organize and write down your answers in your notebook.

3 In small groups, share your personal stories. Use the spidergram or some other visual element in your presentation. Compare your personal stories with your group's stories.

4 Individually, create a "First-Then-Now" poster to represent some changes you have lived through. Then show your poster to your group.

My first school was (name of the school), then I moved to (name of the school)... Nowadays I go to (name of the school).

First	Then	Now

5 Prepare yourself for an oral presentation. Then present your story to your class.

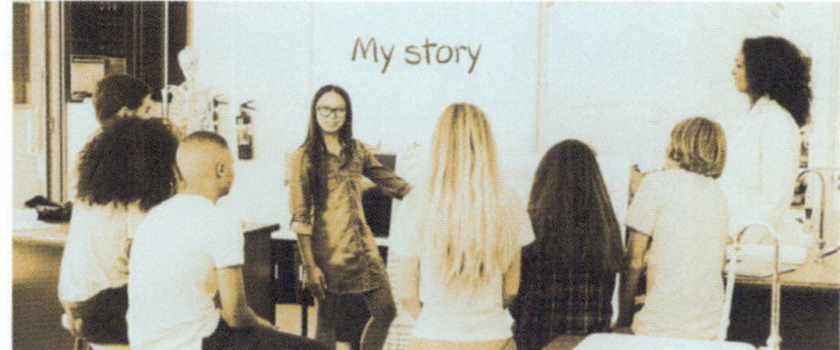

- Study your poster carefully.
- Practice saying the sentences as naturally as possible.
- Look at the audience. Eye contact is very important in oral presentations.
- Make pauses when necessary.

6 Read your classmates' "First-Then-Now" posters. Think of some positive comments you can make about them. Write them in sticky notes and affix them to the posters.

Spark

1 **Do the activities with your classmates.**

a Number what you see in each picture.

- [ ] An autonomous car.
- [ ] Teleportation.
- [ ] A futuristic and sustainable city.
- [ ] A chip in the human brain.

b In your opinion, which pictures show common situations in the future?

____

c What are the advantages and disadvantages of such contexts? Write *A* (advantages) or *D* (disadvantages).

- [ ] Some professions would not be needed anymore (e.g. drivers).
- [ ] There would be fewer traffic accidents.
- [ ] People would exercise less.
- [ ] There would be less garbage.
- [ ] Social divide would be greater.
- [ ] Illnesses could be cured with the installation of a chip.
- [ ] People would commute faster.
- [ ] People would have more free time.

Explore Microblog post

Pre-reading

1 Discuss these questions with your classmates and do the activities.

a Look at the icons and name the social media networks you know.

b Do you use any of these social media networks? What do you use them for?

c Do you follow any accounts on social media network? For example, a person, an organization, a band etc. Do you have any followers yourself?

2 Take a look at this text and answer the questions.

a What kind of text is this? How do you know that?

____

b Where was this text posted?

____

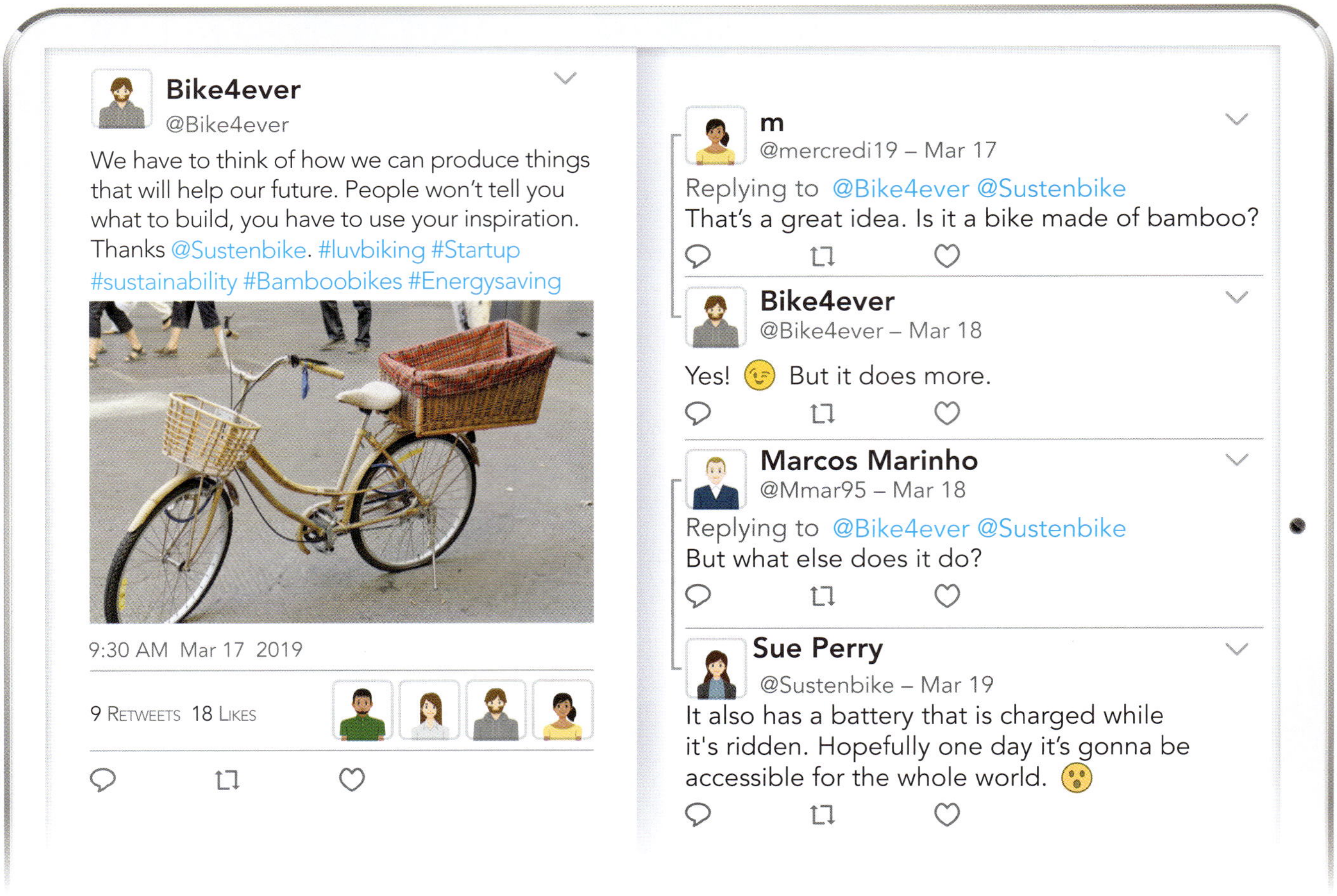

Bike4ever
@Bike4ever
We have to think of how we can produce things that will help our future. People won't tell you what to build, you have to use your inspiration. Thanks @Sustenbike. #luvbiking #Startup #sustainability #Bamboobikes #Energysaving

9:30 AM Mar 17 2019

9 Retweets 18 Likes

m
@mercredi19 – Mar 17
Replying to @Bike4ever @Sustenbike
That's a great idea. Is it a bike made of bamboo?

Bike4ever
@Bike4ever – Mar 18
Yes! 😉 But it does more.

Marcos Marinho
@Mmar95 – Mar 18
Replying to @Bike4ever @Sustenbike
But what else does it do?

Sue Perry
@Sustenbike – Mar 19
It also has a battery that is charged while it's ridden. Hopefully one day it's gonna be accessible for the whole world. 😮

Reading

3 **Read the text in activity 2 and answer the questions.**

a When was this post published?

____

b Match the parts of the tweet to what they mean.

I @Bike4ever @Sustenbike

II #luvbiking #Startup #sustainability

III 18

IV @Bike4ever

[ ] Who posted the message.

[ ] Hyperlinks to other microbloggers mentioned in the post.

[ ] Hyperlinks to popular topics in the microblogging website.

[ ] Number of people who liked the post.

4 **Read the microblog post and the comments in activity 2 again. Then write if the statements are *T* (true) or *F* (false). Justify your answers.**

a [ ] Only Bike4ever replied to the comments.

____

b [ ] Sue Perry explained how the bike works.

____

c [ ] The post got more reposts than likes.

____

d [ ] Sue Perry used formal language in her reply.

____

e [ ] There is no space between the words in the hashtags.

____

5 **Read the following microblog posts. Then check the chart.**

Text 1

Chris
@ceba65
Technology will replace some teachers, but it'll never replace human interaction.
#technology
#LuvTeachers
#Caring-n-sharing
#interaction
2:16 PM – Apr 18 2019
10 Likes

Language clue

#: hashtag
@: "at" symbol

Text 2

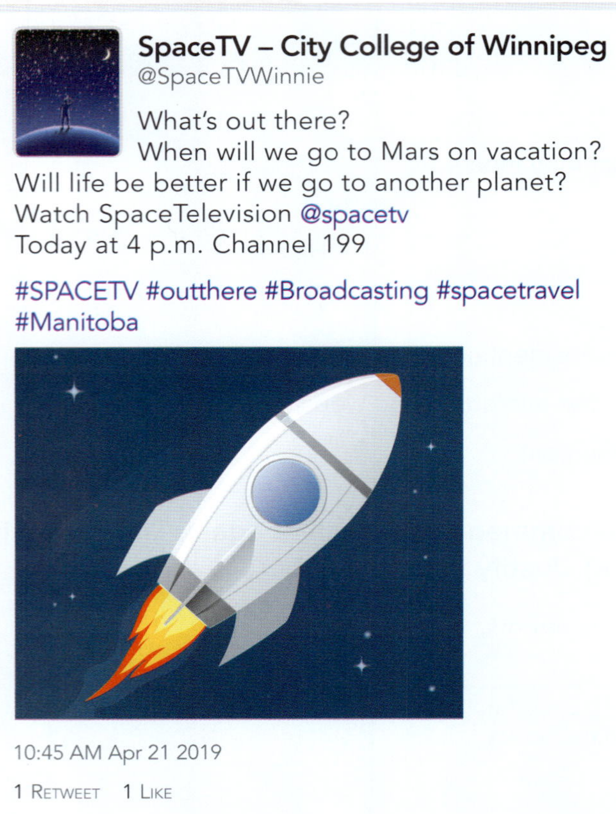

SpaceTV – City College of Winnipeg
@SpaceTVWinnie

What's out there?
When will we go to Mars on vacation?
Will life be better if we go to another planet?
Watch SpaceTelevision @spacetv
Today at 4 p.m. Channel 199

#SPACETV #outthere #Broadcasting #spacetravel #Manitoba

10:45 AM Apr 21 2019

1 Retweet 1 Like

Which microblog post...	Text 1	Text 2
a talks about vacation on another planet?		
b advertises a TV program?		
c expresses the blogger's opinion on technology?		
d is the most popular?		

Post-reading

6 **Read these statements and discuss with a partner if you agree (*A*) or disagree (*D*) with them.**

a ☐ Most people don't care about sustainability.
b ☐ Technology will replace many jobs.
c ☐ Bots will be able to communicate with humans just like real humans.
d ☐ We will live on other planets.

Toolbox Future simple

1 **Look at the icons of social media networks in the "Explore" section. Which platforms would you choose to get information about science and discoveries?**

2 **Analyze these sentences, taken from the microblog posts you read in "Explore". Then check the appropriate options.**

a "We have to think of how we can produce things that will help our future. People won't tell you what to build, you have to use your inspiration."

b "When will we go to Mars on vacation? Will life be better if we go to another planet?"

c "Technology will replace some teachers, but it'll never replace human interaction."

I The highlighted verbs are in the...

☐ past. ☐ present. ☐ future.

II The sentences above express...

☐ orders. ☐ expectations and possibilities for the future.

3 **Based on your answers in activity 2, complete the rules about the use of the future.**

a To make affirmative sentences expressing predictions about the future, we use the auxiliary ______________ before the ______________ in the infinitive.

b The contracted form of "will" in the affirmative form is ______________. The contracted form of "will" in the negative form is ______________ ("will not").

c To make questions, we add ______________ before the subject and use the ______________ in the infinitive.

4 **Read and complete the sentences with the future form of the verbs in parentheses.**

a I ______________ my best to be kind and careful when sharing posts. (try)

b We are very excited to see how this new technology ______________. (turn out)

c Read how a new tool ______________ upper-space lightning. (study)

d Computers ______________ us playing chess, but they ______________ a game! (beat/invent)

Language clue

To beat someone (at a game/ competition): to win
To turn out: to happen in a particular way or to have a particular result

5 **Write predictions about what will happen and what will not happen in the next ten years.**

Building blocks Adverbs to talk about the future

1 Read this post and the replies it received on a discussion forum. Do you agree with one or more of the answers?

Home
Answer
Notifications
Search
In how many years will the smartphone fade away like the desktop PC has?
Charles
Answered Jan 3, 2019 · Author has 24.8k answers and 197.8m answer views
Desktop PC hasn't faded away and probably never will as long as we still use digital tech.
Jessica
Answered Jan 3, 2019 · Author has 37.2k answers and 203.1m answer views
Desktop PC has definitely NOT faded away, but, yes, the current version of smartphones will definitely be obsolete someday in the near future.
Martha
Answered Jan 3, 2019 · Author has 20.4k answers and 50.8m answer views
Future smartphones are likely to become more powerful, but they will never substitute PCs completely.
Ted
Answered Jan 3, 2019 · Author has 43.6k answers and 176.5m answer views
Every new technology will probably be replaced by a better one some day: remember tapes, CDs, floppy disks...

2 Look at the highlighted words in activity 1. Which option completes this statement? Circle the appropriate one.

> Adverbs like "definitely", "never", "probably" and "probably never" **express/don't express** how certain the speaker is about his/her prediction.

3 Read these predictions from an article. How certain are you about them? Rewrite four of its predictions according to your opinion. Use the adverbs from the box.

Predictions for the next 25 years

Experts predict what will happen in the next 25 years:

- We will eradicate malaria.
- We will have effective means for preventing AIDS infection, including a vaccine.
- Any of the imported grain that we do consume will come from genetically modified crops.
- There will be problem-solving games: games in which scientists try to teach gamers real science – how to build proteins to cure cancer, for example.
- We'll see increasing collaboration at work.
- As the web goes mobile, those who pay more will get faster access.
- Technology will be used to create clothes that fit better.
- There will be more automated cars.

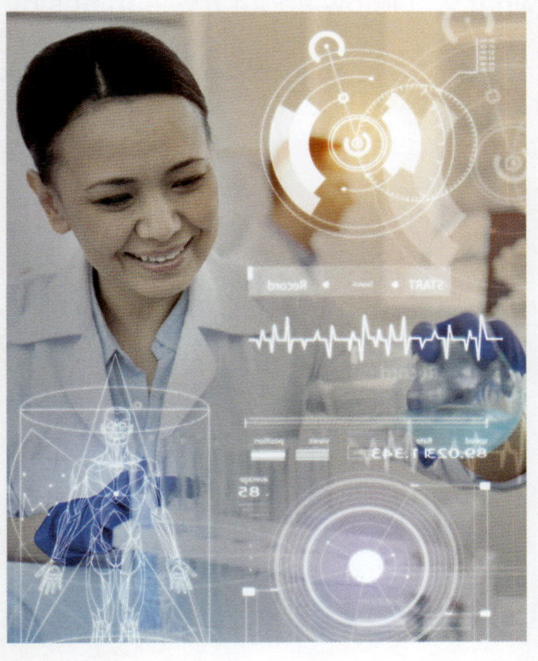

Based on ***The Guardian***, London, January 2, 2011.

definitely **probably** **probably never** **never**

1.

2.

3.

4.

4 Now, tell a partner...

a something you'll probably do next year.

b something you'll definitely do next year.

c something you'll probably never do.

Sync Listening: What does the future hold?

Pre-listening

1 Label the pictures using the words and phrases from the box. Then tell a partner what you know about these things by answering the questions below.

3D printer	colonization of the Moon	nanorobots	wireless battery charger

I

II

III

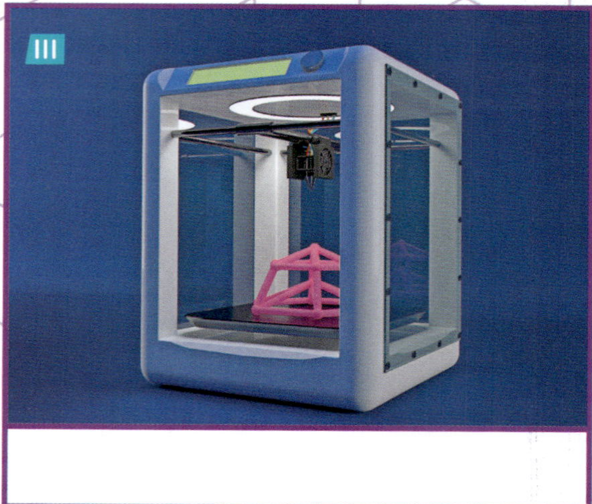

IV

a Which pictures represent technologies that are common nowadays?

______

b Which pictures represent technologies that will probably be common in the future?

______

c In your opinion, when will these technologies be available for most people?

______

Listening

2 2 Listen to the introduction of an audio about the future and underline the appropriate options to complete the text.

> Well, luckily, nowadays you don't have to be a psychic to **predict/imagine** the future. Sometimes it's enough just to analyze the **future/present**. Here are the events that are planned to happen or will probably happen by the year 2030/2050.

3 3 Listen to some predictions about the future. Which of these statements are true, according to the audio? Check the true sentences and rewrite the false one/s to make it/them true.

a ☐ The predictions made are only about technological advances.

____

b ☐ The speaker presents both positive and negative predictions about the future.

____

c ☐ The speaker gives an estimated time for the predictions to become a reality.

____

4 3 Listen to the audio again and choose the appropriate options.

a In 2025, the population of Earth will reach ________ people and there will be ________ more centenarians.

☐ 8 million; 15 times ☐ 18 billion; 50 times ☐ 8 billion; 50 times

b In the same year, electronic devices will be charged using ________ .

☐ Wi-Fi ☐ solar energy ☐ wind energy

c In 2028, the ________ in the Venetian Lagoon will rise, which may make the city uninhabitable.

☐ water level ☐ houses ☐ diseases

d In 2030, the Arctic ________ will have a very small area.

☐ Ocean ☐ ice sheet ☐ iceberg

RTV

Listen to:
Future invention

Post-listening

5 The audio ends with a question. Read it, think about it and tell a partner your answer.

So, which of these predicted future events will you look forward to?

Sync Speaking: Predicting the future

Pre-speaking

1 Discuss these questions with your classmates.

a Which future prediction in this chapter interested you the most? Why?

b In which areas do you think your community/city/country needs more technological advances? Explain.

- [ ] education
- [ ] entertainment
- [ ] food
- [ ] housing
- [ ] medicine
- [ ] sanitation
- [ ] telecommunications
- [ ] transportation
- [ ] others: ______________

c How could you get information about the technological advances that researchers are working on today?

2 Now, prepare a presentation.

a Choose an area from the ones in activity 1, item "b". Research what scientists in this area are developing and what their goals are. Then choose three topics to talk about.

b Review how to make predictions in English and use the script from track 3 to help you, if necessary.

c Prepare a presentation under the title "Top three advances for the future". Remember to include:
- an introduction explaining why you chose these three topics;
- an explanation about each topic;
- the current situation (what scientists are doing, why they are doing that, what already exists etc.);
- what scientists predict for the future (what we will be able to do, how this will impact our lives etc.);
- when this will probably happen;
- your sources.

d Use pictures or videos to illustrate your talk.

e Rehearse your presentation.

Useful language

Do you think we will really have (flying cars) in the next (two) years?
Do you agree that (nanorobots) will (revolutionize medicine)?
Will we really (travel to the Moon) by (2050)?

Speaking

3 Deliver your presentation to your classmates.

a In groups, deliver your presentation.

b Ask your classmates what they think about the predictions you presented. Use the "Useful language" box to help you.

c Listen to your classmates' predictions and express your opinions as well.

Post-speaking

4 Now, discuss these questions with your classmates.

a Why did you choose this area for your presentation?

b What have you learned from your research?

Studio Microblog post

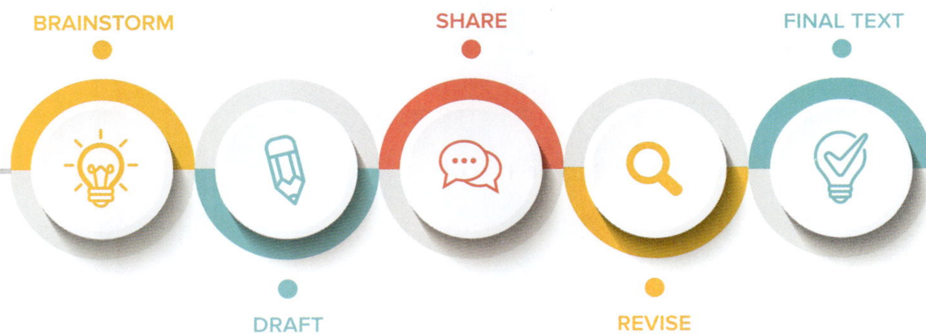

What: a microblog post
To whom: other students; people in general
Media: paper; digital
Objective: express your opinion about the future

1. Review the characteristics of microblog posts and the expressions/vocabulary to talk about the future.
2. Make a list of possible issues about the future and choose one. Look for pictures, media, texts, hashtags etc. related to what you want to discuss about the future.
3. Write a draft of your text with about 280 characters. Use abbreviations. Check if your draft is clear and organized.
4. Share your draft with your classmates and get feedback from them. Make comments on your classmates' texts too.
5. Revise your text according to the feedback you received. Make a clean copy. Draw the layout and include features from the genre, such as speech balloons, arrows to indicate retweets, likes etc. If you want to use a hyperlink or hashtag, use a different color or underline it.
6. Share your final production with your classmates. React to what you read by leaving comments.
7. Make a public display of your texts, organizing them in areas. Discuss if people's views about the future are optimistic, neutral or pessimistic and explain why. Publish your work on the **Students for PEACE Social Media** <www.studentsforpeace.com.br>, using the tag **microblogpost** or others chosen by the students.

Spark

1 Which words can be related to the pictures? Check the appropriate options.

a ☐ aggression
b ☐ allergy
c ☐ balanced diet
d ☐ exercising
e ☐ friendship
f ☐ hydration
g ☐ medical care
h ☐ sadness

2 Use the words you checked in activity 1 to label the pictures. Then share your answers with a partner.

3 **What is the meaning of the word "health" for you? Check the best option.**

a ☐ Health is not being sick.

b ☐ Health is feeling well in all aspects of life.

c ☐ Health is being strong and fit.

4 **Work with a partner. Write down two more things that are necessary for good health.**

____

5 **Do you think it is important for our health to share our emotions and feelings with other people? If so, with whom do you feel safe expressing yourself? Check.**

a ☐ No, I don't think it is important.

b ☐ Yes, I do. I feel safe talking to ______________.

Explore Personal story

Pre-reading

1 **What are some of the feelings you have already felt? Circle them.**

anger anxiety doubt fear insecurity pain sadness worry

2 **Scan the text in activity 3 and check the appropriate options.**

a ☐ It was taken from a magazine.
b ☐ It was taken from the *Teen Ink* website.
c ☐ It is about someone's feelings.
d ☐ It discusses different emotional problems.
e ☐ It is an interview.
f ☐ It is a personal story.

Reading

3 **Read the text and underline two situations that make the writer anxious.**

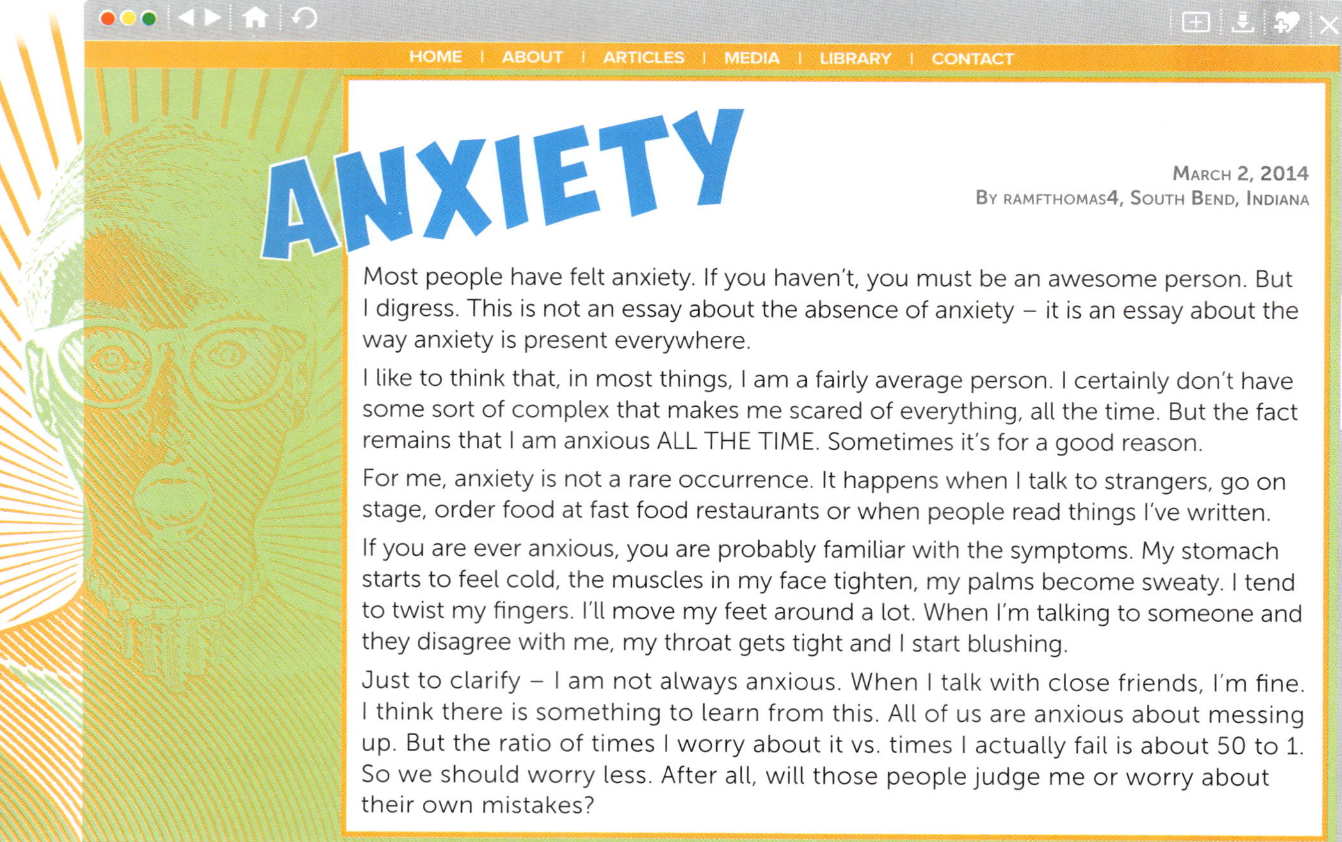

HOME | ABOUT | ARTICLES | MEDIA | LIBRARY | CONTACT

ANXIETY

March 2, 2014
By ramfthomas4, South Bend, Indiana

Most people have felt anxiety. If you haven't, you must be an awesome person. But I digress. This is not an essay about the absence of anxiety – it is an essay about the way anxiety is present everywhere.

I like to think that, in most things, I am a fairly average person. I certainly don't have some sort of complex that makes me scared of everything, all the time. But the fact remains that I am anxious ALL THE TIME. Sometimes it's for a good reason.

For me, anxiety is not a rare occurrence. It happens when I talk to strangers, go on stage, order food at fast food restaurants or when people read things I've written.

If you are ever anxious, you are probably familiar with the symptoms. My stomach starts to feel cold, the muscles in my face tighten, my palms become sweaty. I tend to twist my fingers. I'll move my feet around a lot. When I'm talking to someone and they disagree with me, my throat gets tight and I start blushing.

Just to clarify – I am not always anxious. When I talk with close friends, I'm fine. I think there is something to learn from this. All of us are anxious about messing up. But the ratio of times I worry about it vs. times I actually fail is about 50 to 1. So we should worry less. After all, will those people judge me or worry about their own mistakes?

Adapted from <http://www.teenink.com/opinion/all/article/628674/Anxiety/>. Accessed on February 27, 2019.

4 **Read the text again and number the following ideas in the order they are mentioned by the author.**

a ☐ Symptoms of anxiety.
b ☐ How often the author feels anxious.
c ☐ What the author recommends to people who feel anxiety.
d ☐ What causes anxiety.

5 **Read the sentences and decide if they are *T* (true) or *F* (false) according to the text.**

a ☐ Anxiety is a common feeling.
b ☐ Not many people feel anxiety.
c ☐ The author is different from other people because everybody feels anxiety all the time.
d ☐ The author wants to show readers that we shouldn't worry so much because we don't fail as much as we worry about it.

6 **What are the symptoms of anxiety that the author experiences?**

____

____

7 **The following items present characteristics of a personal story. Which of them apply to the text you read in activity 3?**

The writer...

a ☐ expresses his/her emotions and feelings.
b ☐ is the protagonist and uses first person singular.
c ☐ expresses himself/herself in writing.
d ☐ expresses himself/herself orally.
e ☐ published the story on digital media (blog, social network, forum etc.).
f ☐ published the story in print media (magazine, newspaper etc.).

Post-reading

8 **How do you feel about the text? Check the best option/s for you. Then share your answer/s with your classmates.**

a ☐ The text helped me understand something about myself.
b ☐ I learned about the symptoms of anxiety.
c ☐ I learned about situations that may cause anxiety.

9 **Discuss the questions with your classmates: do you ever feel like the narrator? If so, in which situations?**

____

Toolbox "Some", "any", "many", "much"

1 What kind of health-related issue do these pictures show?

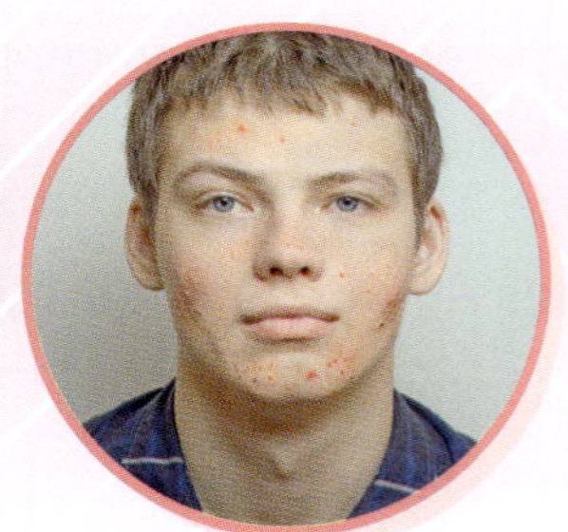

2 Check the statements you think are true about acne. Then read the text to confirm your answers.

a ☐ Acne affects only teenagers.
b ☐ 80% of teenagers have acne.
c ☐ Acne is a normal part of puberty.
d ☐ Hormonal changes don't cause acne.
e ☐ Acne is related to the sebaceous glands.
f ☐ Some lotions and creams can help prevent acne.

Why Do I Get Acne?

HOME | ABOUT | PROGRAMS | MEDIA | CONTACT

If you're a teen, chances are pretty good that you have some acne. Almost 8 in 10 teens have acne, as do many adults.

Teens get acne because of the hormonal changes that come with puberty.

The sebaceous glands in your skin make sebum. Most of the time, the glands make the right amount of sebum, but hormones can stimulate the sebaceous glands to make it in excess.

Pores become clogged if there is too much sebum and too many dead skin cells. Bacteria can then get trapped inside the pores and multiply. This causes swelling and redness — the start of acne.

Is there any way to avoid acne? To help prevent acne, wash your face once or twice a day with a mild soap and warm water.

Make sure to wear "non-comedogenic" or "non-acnegenic" makeup and sunscreen.

Some people find that the oils their skin produces after being in the sun make their pimples worse.

Many lotions and creams containing salicylic acid or benzoyl peroxide are available to help prevent acne and clear it up at the same time. Be sure to follow any label directions about allergy testing.

Based on <https://kidshealth.org/en/teens/acne.html#catpersonal-stories>. Accessed on February 27, 2019.

3 Study the highlighted words in the text in activity 2. Then complete the sentences.

a ________________ is used with countable nouns only, as in ________________, ________________ and ________________.

b ________________ is used with uncountable nouns only, as in ________________.

c ________________ is used in affirmative sentences for both countable – ________________ – and uncountable nouns – ________________.

d ________________ can be used in affirmative sentences with the meaning of "all", as in ________________. It can also be used in questions, as in ________________.

4 Circle the appropriate options to complete the sentences.

a **Many/Much/Any** people show signs of sadness, but only **any/some/many** may be depressed.

b There are **much/many/any** reasons for people to get anxious nowadays.

c There are times when a person doesn't show **much/many/any** symptoms of a cold before having a fever.

d I don't get as **many/much/any** exercise as I should to be healthy.

e Not sleeping well might provoke **some/any/much** reactions, such as irritability and lack of attention.

f The clinical presentation of acne rarely offers **many/much/any** problem to the physician or even to the patient to diagnose. *Acne vulgaris* is the most common form of acne, but there are **much/many/any** uncommon subgroups.

5 Check what you do to take care of your skin.

a ☐

b ☐

c ☐

d ☐

Building blocks Affixes (prefixes and suffixes)

1 **Look at this comic strip. Do you know the name of these two characters? What other characters are part of this comic strip series?**

2 **Now read the comic strip in activity 1 and answer the questions with a partner.**

a How is Lucy feeling in the first frame? Check the best option.

- [ ] She is happy.
- [ ] She is sad.
- [ ] She is curious.

b Which word does Lucy use to create new words in the last frame?

____

c Why do you think Lucy creates all those new words? Check.

- [ ] Because she wants to know where Charlie Brown went.
- [ ] Because she doesn't know the word that means the opposite of "obvious".
- [ ] Because she likes to create new words.

3 **Write *T* (true) or *F* (false) according to the text.**

a ☐ Lucy knows where Charlie Brown is.

b ☐ Linus knows where Charlie Brown is.

c ☐ Linus is worried about Charlie Brown.

Going further

Peanuts is an American comic strip created by Charles M. Schulz. The strip is about a circle of young children. The main character, Charlie Brown, is nervous and lacks self-confidence. Some of the other characters are Woodstock, Snoopy, Franklin, Lucy van Pelt, Linus van Pelt, Marcie, Peppermint Patty and Sally Brown.

Now read this text about eating disorders and do the activity.

WHAT IS AN EATING DISORDER?

It's when someone has an unhealthy focus on eating, exercising or their body size or shape.

Here are some of the most common symptoms.

You may FEEL

- Unhappy with your body shape or size.
- Worried, upset or guilty after eating.
- Moody, irritable or have low energy.
- Nervous or out of control around food.

How you ACT

- Exercise often or excessively.
- Vomit after meals or use laxatives.
- Eat in secret or avoid eating with others.
- Diet, overeat, fast or change the way you eat.

Adapted from <https://kidshelpline.com.au/teens/issues/eating-disorders>. Accessed on February 27, 2019.

Find in the text the words that mean...

a easily irritated: ____________

b easily agitated: ____________

c to eat too much: ____________

d feeling changes in mood: ____________

e feeling guilt: ____________

f in excess: ____________

g not happy: ____________

h not healthy: ____________

i lack of order: ____________

5 **Use the affixes in the box to form words, according to the cues in parentheses. Then, practice asking and answering the questions with a partner.**

-ly	over-	un-	-y

a What do you do when you feel ____________? (not happy)

b Do you consider yourself a ____________ person? (characterized by health)

c Are you ____________ active? (in a physical way)

d How often do you ____________? (sleep too much and not wake up on time)

RTV

Watch: **Prefixes and suffixes**

6 **Read the definition of health according to the World Health Organization (WHO). Then identify and check the healthy habits.**

"HEALTH IS A STATE OF COMPLETE PHYSICAL, MENTAL AND SOCIAL WELL-BEING AND NOT MERELY THE ABSENCE OF DISEASE OR INFIRMITY."

Available at <https://www.who.int/about/who-we-are/constitution>. Accessed on March 6, 2019.

a ☐ I never eat vegetables or fruit.

b ☐ My sister swims two kilometers every day.

c ☐ Jack goes to the dentist twice a year.

d ☐ My father never exercises.

Sync Listening: Talking about health issues

Pre-listening

1 Label the pictures using the words from the box. Then tell a partner what you know about these health-related issues.

ADHD (attention deficit hyperactivity disorder)
allergy   anorexia   asthma   depression   diabetes

a

b

c

d

e

f
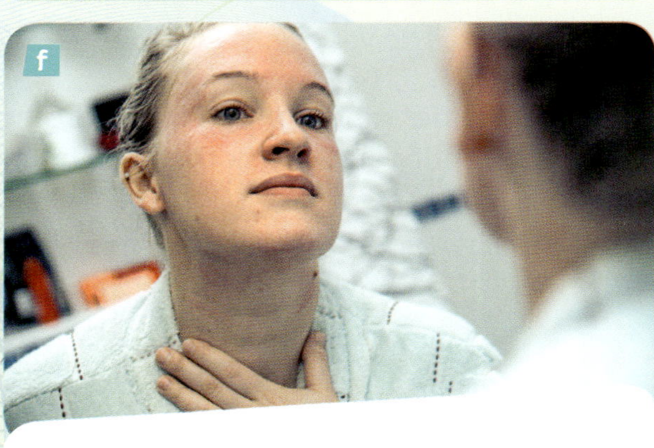

Listening

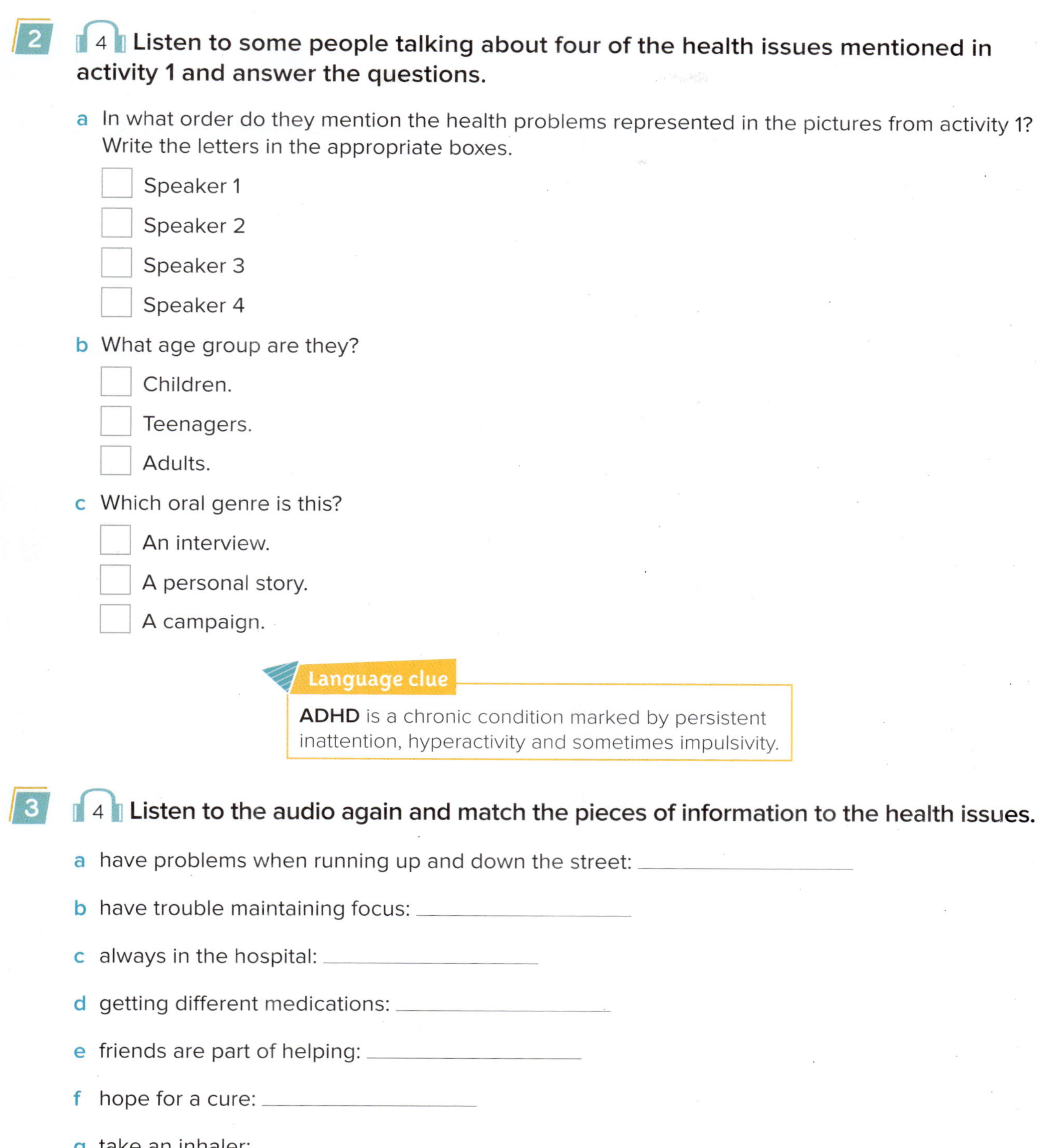

2 4 **Listen to some people talking about four of the health issues mentioned in activity 1 and answer the questions.**

a In what order do they mention the health problems represented in the pictures from activity 1? Write the letters in the appropriate boxes.

- [ ] Speaker 1
- [ ] Speaker 2
- [ ] Speaker 3
- [ ] Speaker 4

b What age group are they?

- [ ] Children.
- [ ] Teenagers.
- [ ] Adults.

c Which oral genre is this?

- [ ] An interview.
- [ ] A personal story.
- [ ] A campaign.

Language clue

ADHD is a chronic condition marked by persistent inattention, hyperactivity and sometimes impulsivity.

3 4 **Listen to the audio again and match the pieces of information to the health issues.**

a have problems when running up and down the street: ____________________

b have trouble maintaining focus: ____________________

c always in the hospital: ____________________

d getting different medications: ____________________

e friends are part of helping: ____________________

f hope for a cure: ____________________

g take an inhaler: ____________________

h end up feeling better after exercising: ____________________

Post-listening

4 **Discuss this question with your classmates: what do you do to keep healthy?**

____

____

Sync Speaking: Personal story

Pre-speaking

1 Look at the picture and check the topics you think may be related to this teenager's story. Then read the text and check your predictions.

a ☐ how he lost weight
b ☐ a balanced diet
c ☐ a therapist
d ☐ running
e ☐ bike riding
f ☐ family support

"I'm Brandon and I'm 17 years old. During my childhood and teen years, I've gained around 140 pounds. I started eating a lot of fast food, and I didn't know how to portion it correctly. Eventually, I had to do something. At that point, I started to ride my bike to school and I lost around 70 pounds. My triggers for overeating are emotional. Before, I used to just sit down and snack, and now I'll call my friends and go out for a bike ride. My family's been very helpful. They've been making sure that I eat correctly. Seeing a doctor is important because you need to make sure you keep the balance between your protein and your carbs. I'm a lot more confident, a lot more open with people and I'm starting to see the person that I want to be."

Adapted from <https://kidshealth.org/en/teens/brandon-vd.html#cattake-care>. Accessed on February 28, 2019.

2 Number the items from 1 to 6 to put the sentences in the order they appear according to Brandon's story.

a ☐ Explaining how the problem happened.
b ☐ Describing how you feel after overcoming the problem.
c ☐ Introducing the situation/problem.
d ☐ Saying how other people helped you.
e ☐ Talking about how you overcame the problem.
f ☐ Introducing yourself.

Speaking

3 Practice talking about a health issue.

Post-speaking

4 Do you agree (*A*) or disagree (*D*) with the following statements?

a ☐ It's easy to talk about health problems.
b ☐ It's helpful to talk about a problem with other people.
c ☐ I trust someone to talk to when I have a problem.

Studio Personal story

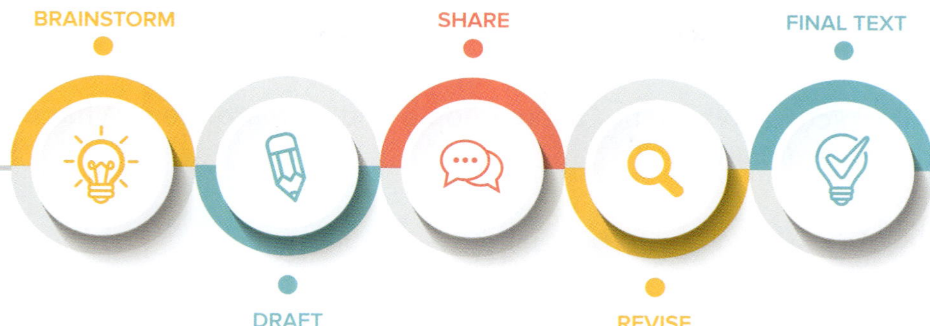

What: a personal story
To whom: classmates
Media: paper; digital
Objective: write about a personal experience

1. What are the objectives of a personal story? Write down some ideas.
2. Think of an experience related to a health issue to share. You can use the texts from pages 22 and 30 as a start.
3. You will need an introduction, a development and a conclusion for your personal story. Make an outline with your main topics for each part.
4. Share your ideas with your classmates and ask for feedback.
5. Write your first draft. Read it. Is it clear? Is it organized? Are the sentences well structured?
6. Make the necessary adjustments. Ask for feedback to your classmates and give it to them.
7. Revise your text and write the final version.
8. Consider the possibility of sharing your story with other people at school.
9. Did you find it interesting to make a personal story? Will it be helpful for other people?
10. Publish your work on the **Students for PEACE Social Media** <www.studentsforpeace.com.br>, using the tag **personalstory** or others chosen by the students.

Peace talk

Chapters 1 and 2
The healing power of laughter

1 Look at the picture. Where are these people and who are they? What do you know about this type of initiative?

2 Read this text, adapted from a book about the work of clown doctors. Then answer the questions.

Is laughter good medicine? Putting humour and health in perspective

Humour and laughter have a positive effect on emotions, physiological processes and pain tolerances.

Laughter affects the mind and the body. There are many reasons why it makes us feel good. Studies show that it enhances immune system functioning and leads to a reduction of stress hormones in the body. In addition, a recent study found that humour and laughter trigger the brain's reward centres.

The effects of humour and laughter on physical discomfort have also been studied. An examination of the impact of stress on inflammatory disorders, asthma, cancer and heart disease suggests that humour can improve prognosis in these situations.

Other studies have shown that laughter reduces pain and that a relaxation response is experienced after it.

Adapted from WARREN, Bernie; SPITZER, Peter. ***Smiles are Everywhere:* Integrating Clown-Play into Healthcare Practice.** New York: Routledge, 2014. p. 4.

a Does the use of humor in treatments have some type of scientific background? Justify your answer with an excerpt of the text.

b After reading the text, do you think the work of clown doctors is important? Why?

Going further

Research the presence of clown doctors in different countries. What are the benefits of their work? What challenges do they face?

3 **Look at the poster and follow the instructions.**

a Work in pairs. Suppose you were invited to contribute with a poster, like the one in the example, to help cheer someone up and make him/her feel better. Think of inspirational phrases that could help someone feel better. Take notes.

b Choose one of the phrases to create your poster and look for one or more pictures to illustrate it.

c Make your poster.

d Decide where your poster will be displayed (in the classroom, in the school hall etc.).

3 Time to celebrate!

1 2 4

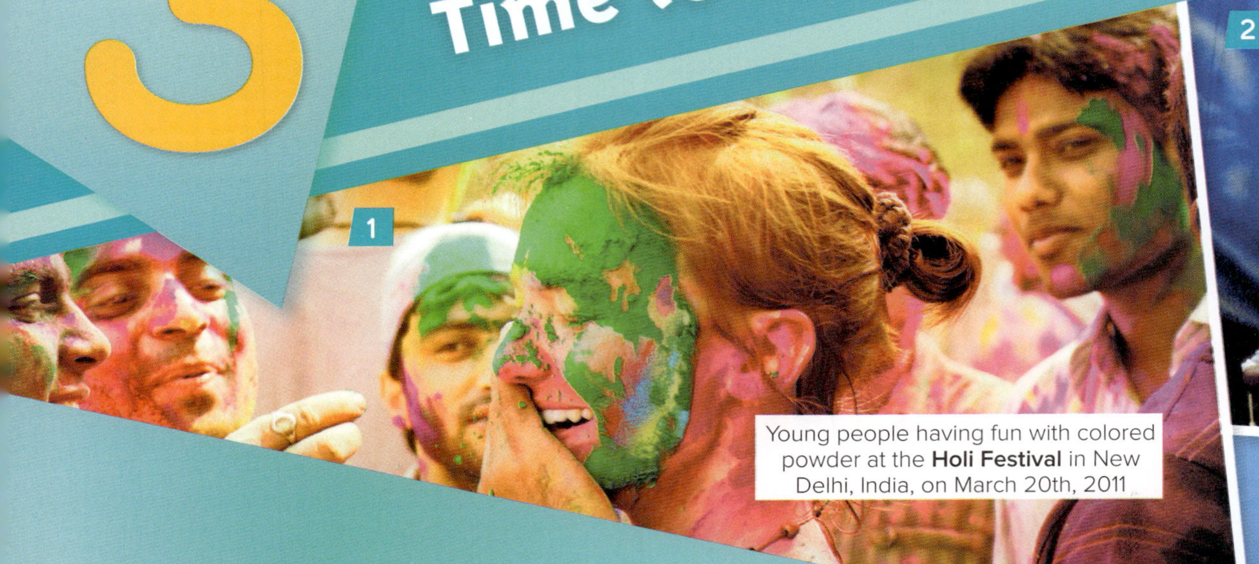

Young people having fun with colored powder at the **Holi Festival** in New Delhi, India, on March 20th, 2011

Goals

- Get to know and explore celebrations related to the English language as well as to other languages, recognizing the diversity among different cultures.
- Make an oral presentation about traditional/folk songs.
- Reflect on the importance of understanding the historical reasons behind celebrations.
- Review the present simple in the affirmative, negative and interrogative forms.
- Understand an oral presentation about the history of traditional Irish songs.
- Understand and produce an informational text about celebrations.
- Understand and use the names of the months.
- Understand the use of ordinal numbers in dates.

1 Look at the pictures and discuss the questions with your classmates.

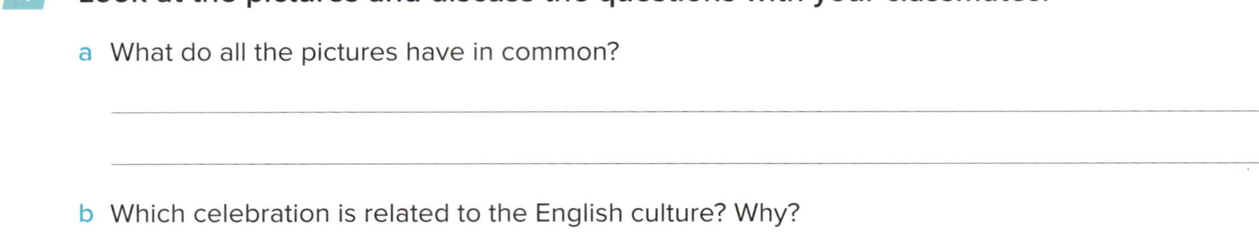

a What do all the pictures have in common?

____

____

b Which celebration is related to the English culture? Why?

____

____

An inflatable globe and a windmill serve as visual props in encouraging ecology at an **Earth Day** celebration in Washington D.C., U.S., on April 22nd, 1990

Celebration of the **Inti Raymi** (Inca Festival of the Sun) at the Sacsayhuamán Fortress, in Cusco, Peru, on June 24th, 2012

Crowd celebrating the **New Year** in Shanghai, China, on January 24th, 2017

People wearing masks during a traditional **Shakespeare Day** parade through the streets of Stratford-upon-Avon, England, on April 23rd, 2016

c Do you know any of these celebrations? If so, which one/s?

____

____

d Would you like to take part in any of these celebrations? If so, which one/s?

____

____

Going further

Research celebrations around the world. Then choose one and share your findings with your classmates.

Explore Informational text

Pre-reading

1 **Scan texts 1 and 2 and answer the questions orally.**

a Where were the texts published?

____

b What are both texts about?

____

____

c Which text looks more attractive to you? Why?

____

____

Text 1

India's colorful Holi festival

March 2nd, 2018, 5:13 PM By Radhika Chalasani

Students with colored powder on their faces dance as they celebrate the Hindu festival of Holi, announcing spring, at a university campus in Chandigarh, India, on March 1st, 2018

Vibrant colors envelope India when Hindus celebrate the end of winter and the arrival of spring with the annual festival of Holi. Also known as the festival of colors, (a) it is a time to let go of certain social norms by wearing all-white clothes to dance and douse friends, family and strangers in colored powders or water of deep tones of magenta, blue, green, yellow or orange. Holi has its roots in stories from the Indian mythology. Though the official date this year is March 2nd, (b) different parts of the country celebrate it on the day before or over several days.

Adapted from <https://abcnews.go.com/International/indias-colorful-holi-festival/story?id=53470604>. Accessed on February 21, 2019.

Text 2

WHAT ARE HOLI COLORS, AND WHAT GIVES THEM SUCH VIBRANT TONES?

By Jessica Marshall

"Modern synthetic chemistry has shown that a lot of colors are available for pretty cheap prices," Michael Rajamathi, a chemist at St. Joseph's College Autonomous, says. But there is still a cost. Some Indian powders may contain toxic, metal-based pigments.

One report from a dermatology clinic in India detailed skin lesions, burning and eye irritation among health problems resulting from playing Holi.

Demand for safe colors, including a return to plant-based Holi colors, has spread. At the Council of Scientific & Industrial Research's National Botanical Research Institute in Lucknow, India, a team developed herbal colored powders that are now in commercial production.

Adapted from ***What's That Stuff?*** Chemical & Engineering News. American Chemical Society Issue. February 26, 2018. Volume 96, Issue 9. p. 28-29.

Reading

2 **Read texts 1 and 2. Then write if the statements refer to text 1 (*T1*) or text 2 (*T2*).**

a The author includes scientific facts in the text.	
b The author explains the reason why people celebrate the date.	
c The author gives a visual idea of how participants interact during the event.	
d The author mentions the opinions of specialists.	

3 **Read the highlighted extracts "a" and "b" in text 1 and make inferences based on the context. Then check the appropriate options.**

a What do people in Indian culture usually do in their daily lives?

- [ ] People probably obey social norms and wear clothes with different colors.
- [ ] People normally like to throw powder on others.

b When is Holi celebrated in India?

- [ ] There isn't a specific date to celebrate Holi.
- [ ] Holi is always celebrated on March 2nd.

Post-reading

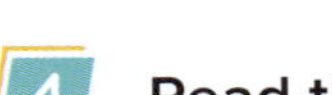

4 **Read these questions. Then discuss them with your classmates.**

a Text 2 shows a different perspective of the festival compared to text 1. How can you compare both?

b In general, informative texts about festivals do not mention the risks involved in the events. Why is that?

Building blocks Months and ordinal numbers

1 **Read these captions of pictures from the chapter. Then match the highlighted parts to their equivalent word forms.**

I Crowd celebrating the New Year in Shanghai, China, on January 24th, 2017

II An inflatable globe and a windmill serve as visual props in encouraging ecology at an Earth Day celebration in Washington D.C., U.S., on April 22nd, 1990

III People wearing masks during a traditional Shakespeare Day parade through the streets of Stratford-upon-Avon, England, on April 23rd, 2016

IV Young people having fun with colored powder at the Holi Festival in New Delhi, India, on March 20th, 2011

V Students with colored powder on their faces dance as they celebrate the Hindu festival of Holi, announcing spring, at a university campus in Chandigarh, India, on March 1st, 2018

a ☐ first
b ☐ twenty-fourth
c ☐ twentieth
d ☐ twenty-second
e ☐ twenty-third

2 **Now, complete the sentences based on activity 1.**

a Items ______________________ contain ordinal numbers written in an abbreviated format (cardinal number + two-letter suffix).

b The two-letter suffixes used in ordinal numbers are ______________________.

c Items ______________________ contain ordinal numbers in word forms (not abbreviated).

d The rule to use ordinal numbers is: for numbers that end in 1, use ______________________; for numbers that end in 2, use ______________________; for numbers that end in 3, use ______________________; and for other numbers, use ______________________.

3 **Read the names of the months of the year. Then circle the months mentioned in this chapter.**

January	February	March	April
May	June	July	August
September	October	November	December

Going further

In English, dates are written in two ways:

month/day/year: 12/1/2023 ⇒ **December 1st, 2023**

day/month/year: 1/12/2023 ⇒ the **1st** of **December 2023**

Toolbox Present simple (review)

1 **Look at the picture and read the text. Then answer the questions.**

Raksha Bandhan

Raksha Bandhan is a holiday that celebrates the relationship between brothers and sisters. But that doesn't mean just blood relationships. It is also celebrated among cousins, sister and sister-in-law, aunt and nephew, and other relations.

When do people celebrate it?

The occasion of Raksha Bandhan is celebrated on the full moon day of the Hindu lunisolar calendar in the month of Shravana, which typically falls in August.

What do people do?

A sister ties decorated silk around her brother's right wrist and gives him *tika* (a red mark on the forehead). Brothers give sisters gifts, like jewelry or new clothes, and promise to make sure the sister is always taken care of. If his sister is married, a brother may need to travel many miles to share this day with her.

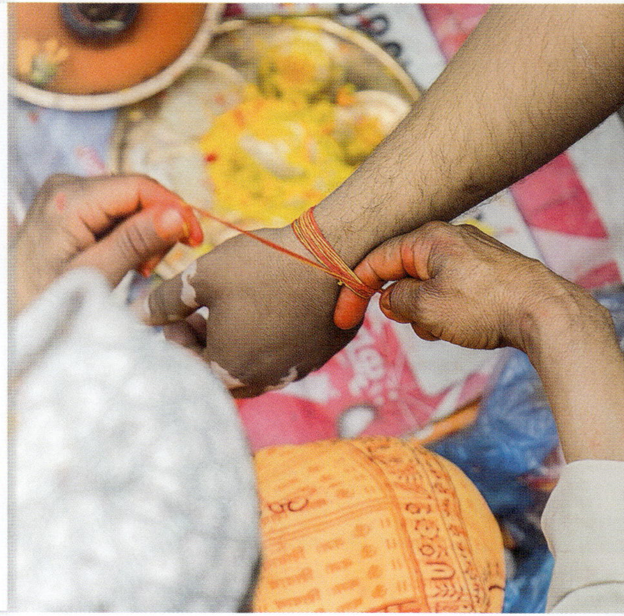

Based on YACKLEY-FRANKEN, Nicki. ***Teens in Nepal.*** Minneapolis: Compass Point Books, 2008.

a What is Raksha Bandhan? How do people celebrate it?

____

____

____

b Do you think it would be interesting to have a similar holiday in your country? Why?

____

2 **Look at the text in activity 1 again. Then do the activities.**

a Considering the highlighted sentences, it is possible to say that we use the present simple to...

- [ ] talk about an action in the past.
- [ ] talk about a habitual action.

b The verbs "falls", "ties" and "gives" are...

- [ ] in the 3rd person singular (-s).
- [ ] in the 3rd person plural.

c The interrogative sentence/s in the present simple in the text is/are:

____

d Circle the options that complete the basic structure of the present simple in the interrogative form.

(*Wh-* word +) **"do" or "does"/"did"** + subject + **main verb in the past simple/main verb in the infinitive**.

3 Read the excerpt about a special date and answer the questions.

World Environment Day 2018: things you were doing that harm the environment
Using plastic bags
"Avoiding the usage of plastic in any forms" is one of the basic and important changes we need to adapt to. Plastic in any form is hazardous as it doesn't decay. Plastic bags and bottles don't biodegrade and no one knows how long it takes until they're completely gone.

Adapted from <http://www.freepressjournal.in/webspecial/world-environment-day-2018-10-things-you-didnt-know-you-were-doing-that-harms-the-environment/1289931>. Accessed on February 22, 2019.

a What special date does the excerpt mention?

____

____

b To avoid harming the environment, what is one action the text suggests doing?

____

____

c Besides avoiding plastic bags, how can people celebrate it? Circle what would be good possibilities in your opinion. Explain the reasons to your classmates.

collecting trash from the beach/parks/streets **going to concerts**
making flyers **making posters** **participating in parades**
planting trees **promoting bike rides**

d The negative sentence/s in the present simple in the text is/are:

____

____

e The basic structure of the present simple in the negative form is:

Subject + ______________________________ + main verb in the infinitive.

Sync Listening: Traditional folk music

Pre-listening

1 **Look at the pictures. Then number the sentences accordingly.**

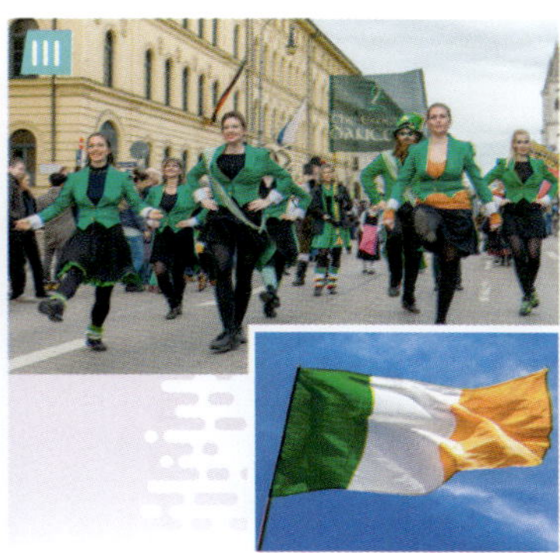

______________ ______________ ______________

a ☐ Australian aboriginal dance.

b ☐ Irish step dance.

c ☐ American square dance.

Listening

2 5 **Listen to extracts of three different folk songs and number the pictures in activity 1.**

3 6 **Listen to the introduction of an audio about a type of music related to one of the dance performances in activity 1. Then complete the sentences.**

a The country it refers to is ______________________________.

b The audio is about the ______________________________.

c The information is given in the format of a ______________________________.

4 7 **Listen to the entire audio and circle the correct alternatives.**

a The Celts came to Ireland around **the first century BC/the first century AD**.

b The Celts brought with them culture and music from **Eastern Europe/Western Europe**.

c The Celts had been heavily influenced by the cultures in Asia and in **Central Africa/ North Africa**.

d The fiddle that the Celts used was **exactly the same as our modern violin/very different from our modern violin**.

e The human voice **was a very important part of traditional Irish music/was a minor element in traditional Irish music**.

5 7 Besides the fiddle and the violin, five of the following musical instruments are mentioned in the audio. Listen again and check the one that was not mentioned.

Post-listening

6 Do the activities with a partner.

a The voice is an important characteristic of ______ ______ ______ ______ ______ traditional songs because it tells a ______ ______ ______ ______ ______.

b Can you name some musical instruments that are used in folk songs in Brazil?

____

Sync Speaking: A brief history of some types of folk music

Pre-speaking

1 What do you remember from the audio in the previous section? Complete the paragraph.

It is about the history of traditional ______________________ music. This type of music came to Ireland with an ancient people called the ______________________. Some of the instruments related to this type of music are ____.

Another important element in this type of traditional music is the ____________________________.

Going further

Ireland is deeply influenced by the Celtic culture. Other countries were also inhabited by the Celts, such as Scotland and Wales. The Celts were a very important civilization. They were responsible for the spread of iron metallurgy, for example.

2 Now, prepare a presentation about a brief history of some types of folk music. Follow these steps.

a Choose some type of folk/traditional music related to any English-speaking country.

b Search for information about it.

c Write the script for your presentation. Use the organization of the script from the "Sync – Listening" section as a reference.

d Share your script with some classmates to get their feedback.

e Use visual aids to make your presentation clearer.

Useful language

Introducing: *Hey, there/Hello, folks/Hi, everyone. I'll make a quick presentation on the history of...*

Presenting the facts: *It all started when/with/because...; Some/One of the most popular/common musical instrument/s in this type of music is/are...; Other important element/s in this type of music is/are...; In this type of music, people usually...*

Conclusion: *So, that was a very brief presentation on the history of.../So, that ends my presentation on... Thanks for watching/listening./Thanks for your time./Thank you for your attention.*

Speaking

3 **Get ready to present the information you collected to your classmates. Follow the steps.**

a If possible, rehearse your presentation in front of a mirror. When you use the right gestures and facial expressions, you improve your presentation and your audience responds better. Body language plays an important role in communicating with people. Look at some habits you should avoid.

I Folding arms

What you communicate:

- You are not enthusiastic about your presentation.
- You are not open to your audience.
- You are uncomfortable in the presence of your audience.

II Resting hands on hips (akimbo)

What you communicate:

- You are angry or irritated.
- You want to appear bigger by taking more space.
- You are ready for action in an authoritative way.

III Putting hands in the pockets

What you communicate:

- You are nervous and you want to hide it.
- You are uninterested in what you are doing.
- You are unsure of yourself.

IV Crossing legs

What you communicate:

- You are insecure and tense.
- You are unfamiliar with your audience.
- You are not very receptive.

b What should you do instead? Circle the tips that you find useful.

face the audience	make eye contact	move around the space
smile at the audience	stand straight	vary your gestures
	walk while speaking	

c Start your presentation.

Post-speaking

4 **Discuss these questions.**

a In your opinion, were you able to use body language appropriately in your presentation?

b What have you learned from your classmates' presentations?

Studio Informational text

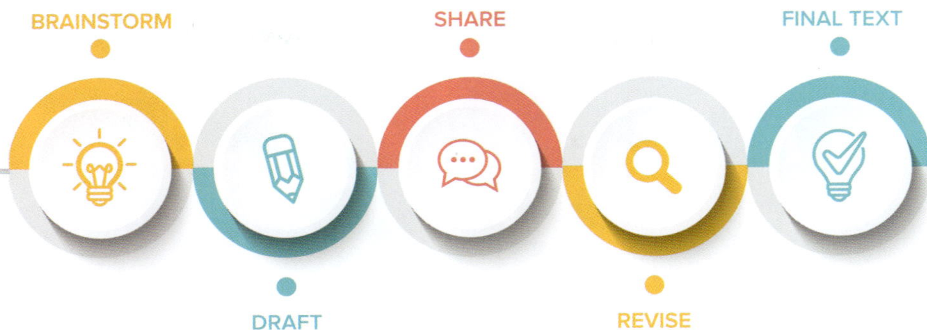

What: an informational text
To whom: other students; the school community
Media: paper; digital
Objective: historically rescue the meaning of a local, national or international celebration

1. Make a list of the characteristics of an informational text.
2. Choose a celebration. It can be a local, national or international one. Look for information about it on the internet, in libraries or even with other people.
3. Try to answer some questions about the event: when, how and why is it celebrated? Who takes part in it?
4. Organize your answers in paragraphs using the vocabulary from this unit.
5. Read your text. Check if it is organized and has well-structured sentences. Is it clear? Is it adequate for your public?
6. Share your draft with your classmates. Give and receive feedback.
7. Revise your text and, if necessary, rewrite it based on the feedback received.
8. Share your text again, this time in small groups.
9. Now, organize a bulletin board with the information on the celebrations the class has chosen.
10. Publish your work on the **Students for PEACE Social Media** <www.studentsforpeace.com.br>, using the tag **informationaltext** or others chosen by the students.

____

____

____

____

4 Art

Museu de Arte de São Paulo Assis *Chateaubriand* (1947), by Lina Bo Bardi. Architecture, 11,000 m^2. São Paulo, Brazil

Self-Portrait with Bandaged Ear (1889), by Vincent van Gogh. Oil on canvas, 60 cm x 49 cm. Courtauld Gallery, London, England

Goals

- Describe and compare works of art.
- Develop aesthetic fluency.
- Recognize different kinds of art, especially visual ones.
- Reflect on the role of art as an agent of change in society.
- Understand and create an audio guide describing a work of art.
- Understand and use the comparative form of adjectives.
- Understand informational texts about art.

Spark

1 Discuss the question and do the activity with your classmates.

a Look at the pictures. What do they have in common?

____

b Match the pictures to their descriptions.

- [ ] A museum that keeps works of art and is itself a work of art.
- [ ] A self-portrait of a famous artist.
- [ ] An architectural monument.
- [ ] A sculpture of children playing by a river.
- [ ] A photograph of elephant seals.

3

First Generation (2000), by Chong Fah Cheong. Bronze sculpture. Singapore River Bank, Singapore, Singapore

4

Arch of Titus (AD 82). Architecture, 15.4 m x 13.5 m. Palatium, Rome, Italy

5

Southern Elephant Seal Calves, Saint Andrew's Bay, South Georgia (2009), by Sebastião Salgado. Photography, 61 cm x 88.9 cm. Silver Gelatin Print. Huxley-Parlour, London, England

2 Read the labels of the artwork and the following descriptions. Then write which artwork the descriptions refer to.

a It is situated in São Paulo. ______

b It was painted with oil paint. ______

c It pictures animals in their habitat. ______

d It is more than 1,000 years old. ______

e This artwork is installed next to a river. ______

Explore Informational text about a work of art

Pre-reading

1 **Make a quick interview with your classmates. Find someone who...**

a likes to take pictures. ____________________

b smiles when has his/her picture taken. ____________________

c makes picture albums. ____________________

d only posts pictures on the internet. ____________________

e hates to take pictures. ____________________

f loves special effects on pictures. ____________________

g has a professional camera. ____________________

h wants to take a course in photography. ____________________

2 **Look at the pictures in activity 4 and check the characteristics you can see in them.**

- [ ] black and white
- [ ] bright colors
- [ ] different focus
- [ ] outdoor scenery
- [ ] something to reflect on
- [ ] complex technique
- [ ] unusual theme
- [ ] other: ____________

3 **Look at the pictures in activity 4 again and check.**

a Based on the pictures, the text is about...

- [ ] poverty.
- [ ] childhood games.
- [ ] war and migration.

b Which adjectives can you use to describe the children in the pictures?

- [ ] serious
- [ ] happy
- [ ] calm
- [ ] mysterious
- [ ] nervous
- [ ] brave

Reading

4 Now read the text. Check the appropriate sentences.

ART | CHILDREN OF WAR

They have no home, sometimes no parents, and their future is uncertain. But Sebastião Salgado's photographs capture them in a moment of peace.

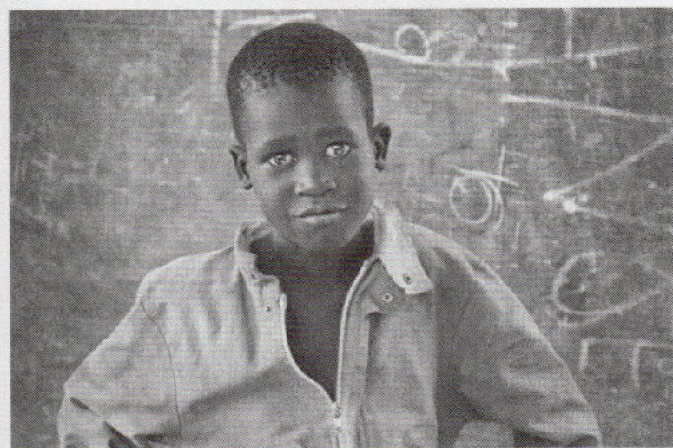

Around half the world's 50 million refugees are children under the age of 18, according to the United Nations High Commission for Refugees. Forced away from their homes – and in many cases from their parents – by war, they live in horrible conditions in camps and orphanages, where they are vulnerable to disease and recruitment as soldiers.

Sebastião Salgado, who has photographed migrant populations around the world for decades, says that children suffer most from being displaced, but they rarely show it. They are the ones who approach him first, smiling and waving, crowding to get into the picture.

"Wherever I went, I was surrounded. Finally, I said to them, 'I'm going to sit here. If you want me to take a picture of you, line up.'"

Photographing them individually, Salgado could catch something of each child's personality. The pictures were calmer, and more candid for it. "For a brief moment," he says, "they were able to say 'I am'."

Adapted from ***The Guardian***, London, February 1, 2003.

a ☐ The photographs were taken in a natural catastrophe situation.

b ☐ Salgado prefers not to take pictures of the children in groups.

c ☐ The children are alone in the pictures because they asked for privacy.

d ☐ Salgado mentions a contrast: children suffer a lot because of the war, but they do not show their feelings as adults do.

e ☐ The children like cameras, but they don't want to be photographed.

Going further

Visit art museums online and choose one. What kinds of art does it exhibit? Is there accessibility to the museum and its collections? Share your findings with your classmates.

Post-reading

5 Art has had different functions throughout history. What do you think the purpose/s of Salgado's art is/are? Check your option/s. Then compare your answer/s to your classmates'.

☐ To express the imagination.

☐ To denounce something wrong.

☐ To have therapeutic purpose.

☐ To communicate something.

☐ To have religious purpose.

Toolbox Comparative adjectives

1 In pairs, read the comic strip and the cartoon and choose the appropriate options.

Text 1

Text 2

a In text 1...

- [ ] Ernie and his friend wanted to be frogs.
- [ ] the art director took revenge on Ernie and his friend.

b In text 2...

- [ ] the statue can't think.
- [ ] the statue is bored and would like to move.

Going further

Look at this sculpture called *The Thinker*, by French sculptor Auguste Rodin. Then look at text 2 again. What do they have in common? What is funny about the cartoon?

The Thinker (1880), by Auguste Rodin. Bronze sculpture, 71.5 cm x 36.4 cm x 59.5 cm. National Gallery of Art, Washington, United States.

2 Read texts 1 and 2 again. Then circle the appropriate options.

a In text 1, one of the characters believes that **writers/art directors** are more sensitive than **writers/art directors**.

b In text 1, the adjective that makes the comparison is **sensitive/ridiculous**.

c In text 2, the character thinks that being a **dancer/thinker** is more fun than being a **dancer/thinker**.

d In text 2, the expression used in the comparison is **a lot more fun/more fun**.

3 Take a look at these examples and check the appropriate sentences.

The pictures were calmer, and more candid for it.

His first painting is better than the new one.

A lot of people think it is easier to take pictures with digital cameras.

Going to a museum is more interesting than going shopping, for sure!

a ☐ The highlighted adjectives are in the comparative form.

b ☐ "Calmer" and "more interesting" follow the same rule.

c ☐ "Better" is the comparative of "good".

d ☐ "More candid" and "more interesting" follow the same rule.

Language clue

Fun is irregular, so the comparative is **more fun**.
Better is the comparative of **good**.
Worse is the comparative of **bad**.
Farther/Further is the comparative of **far**.

4 Now, complete the chart with the adjectives in the box.

calm candid easy fun good interesting sensitive

COMPARATIVE FORM			
short adjective + *-er*	*more* + long adjective	*more* + short adjective	irregular

5 Look at the chart in activity 4. Complete the rules about the comparatives.

- We add ________ to most one-syllable or two-syllable adjectives to make their comparative form.
- We change *y* to ________ before adding the ending ________ to the adjective to make their comparative form.
- We use ________ before adjectives with two syllables or more to make their comparative form.

Going further

For comparisons of equality, we use *as* + adjective + *as*. For example: *Vincent van Gogh was* **as talented as** *Auguste Rodin*.

Building blocks Kinds of art

1 Look at the pictures and name each art form. Use words from the box to help you. Not all the words will be used.

cinema craft dance installation painting theater

2 Look at the works of art in activity 1 and discuss these questions in pairs.

a What kinds of art do you like? Do you have a favorite one?

b Do you know the other kinds of art from the box? Which ones?

Look at these works of art and their corresponding reinterpretations. Then, in pairs, use the adjectives from the box to compare them.

curious	dark	delicate	dramatic	
impressive	interesting	light	sad	shocking

1

The Death of Marat (1793), by Jacques-Louis David. Oil on canvas, 162 cm x 128 cm. Oldmasters Museum, Brussels, Belgium

Marat (Sebastião) (2008), by Vik Muniz. Digital C-print, 76.7 cm x 59.7 cm. Museum of Arts and Design, New York, United States

The Scream (1893), by Edvard Munch. 91 cm x 73.5 cm. National Gallery and Munch Museum, Oslo, Norway

Homage to the Scream (2006), by Mark Langan. Cardboard, 71 cm x 78 cm. Private collection

Useful language

What do you mean?
I'm sorry, I didn't understand. Can you explain that again, please?
Why do you think so?
I mean...
What I want to say is...

Sync Listening: Audio guides in museums

Pre-listening

1 **Look at the paintings and talk about them with your classmates.**

1

2

a Have you ever seen these paintings before? Do you know who painted them?

b Look at the paintings again and check the best statements.

- [ ] In both pictures the person is sitting.
- [ ] Both pictures show an indoor scene.
- [ ] The person in picture 1 is sitting on a couch.
- [ ] The person in picture 2 is looking at a house.

2 **Now work in pairs. Look at the paintings in activity 1 again and try to guess their names and painters.**

Christina's World – Andrew Wyeth (1948) ____________________

The Dream – Henri Rousseau (1910) ____________________

Listening

3 🎧 8 **Listen to the first part of two audio guides from MoMA (The Museum of Modern Art) and complete the statements with the number of the paintings in activity 2.**

a The first audio guide describes painting ☐.

b The second audio guide describes painting ☐.

4 🎧 8 **Listen again. Then choose the appropriate option.**

a According to the first audio, ...

☐ the woman in the painting was the artist's neighbor.

☐ the artist didn't know the woman in the painting.

b The first audio informs us that the house that appears in the background...

☐ belonged to the artist, Andrew Wyeth. ☐ belonged to Christina.

c According to the second audio, ...

☐ people should take a close look at the painting in order to appreciate it.

☐ people should interact with the work of art as if they were in the jungle too.

d The second audio mentions...

☐ the lion, the bird and the elephant. ☐ the musician, the woman and the lion.

5 🎧 9 **Now listen to the second part of the audio guides and match the two halves of sentences.**

a According to the first audio, the woman is alone on the ground because...

b The artist decided to portray Christina in one of his paintings because...

c According to the second audio, the sofa in the jungle...

d According to the second audio, the artist used as an inspiration for a painting...

☐ he thought she was brave and strong and decided to honor her with a painting.

☐ seems to represent a dream.

☐ she wasn't able to walk, but she didn't want to use crutches or a wheelchair, so she crawled on the ground.

☐ zoos, city gardens, museums and his imagination.

Going further

Find out more about these and other works of art at MoMA (https://www.moma.org/).

Post-listening

6 **Discuss these questions in small groups.**

a If you were Christina, would you refuse to use crutches or a wheelchair?

b Have you ever had a weird dream like the one in *The Dream*? If so, how did you feel?

Sync Speaking: Creating an audio guide

Pre-speaking

1 **In your opinion, why are audio guides important?**

- [ ] They can help people who are visually impaired when visiting a museum.
- [ ] Some people need to know more details to appreciate the work of art.
- [ ] Some people like to know the meaning of the artwork.
- [ ] Other: ____________________

2 **Do you have a favorite work of art? Select at least one. If you don't have one, do some research in order to find one that you can describe in an audio guide.**

3 **Which information do you think should be mentioned when describing a work of art to museum visitors? Check at least 4 of them.**

- [ ] name of the artist
- [ ] date of creation
- [ ] materials used
- [ ] why it is important
- [ ] where you can see it
- [ ] which art movement it belongs to

Speaking

4 **Now you are going to describe the work of art you have selected. Work in pairs and follow the instructions.**

a Do some research in English on the work of art. Use the information in activity 3.

b What other details about this artwork are important?

c Write a brief script to help you and practice your presentation with your partner.

d If possible, record your presentation in order to make a descriptive audio guide like the one in the "Sync – Listening" section. Create a poster or a slide with a picture of the work of art.

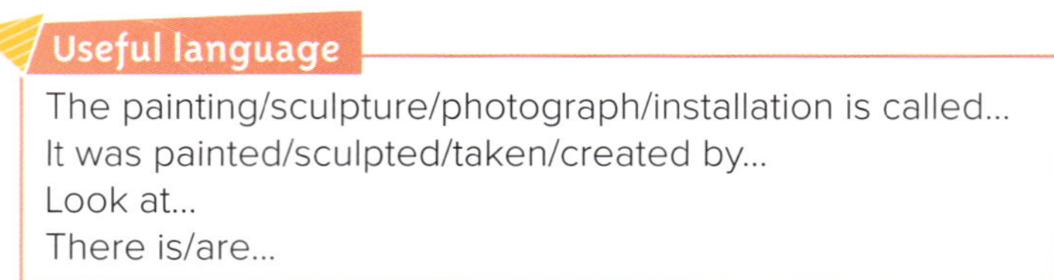

Useful language

The painting/sculpture/photograph/installation is called...
It was painted/sculpted/taken/created by...
Look at...
There is/are...

Post-speaking

5 **Discuss these questions with your classmates.**

a Do you think it was challenging to make a description of the artwork?

b Which was your favorite presentation in class? Why?

Studio Comparing art

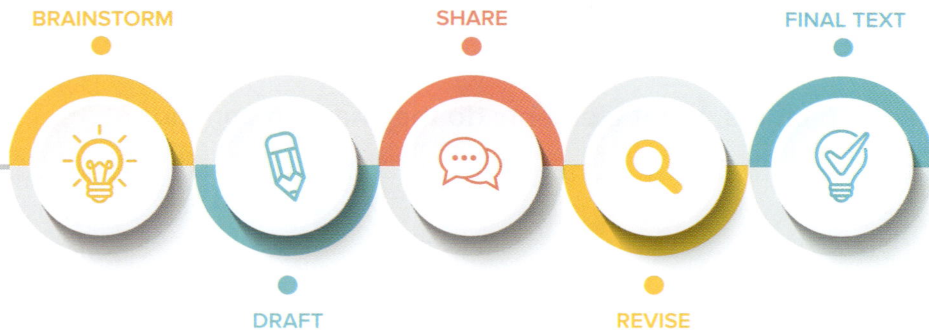

What: an informational text comparing works of art
To whom: other students; the school community
Media: paper; digital
Objective: compare two works of art (the original and its reinterpretation)

1. Write a text about a reinterpretation of art for a school exhibit. In pairs, choose two works of art (the original and its reinterpretation) and look for the information you need, such as artists, dates and places where they were made etc.
2. Analyze the two pieces. How do they differ/look alike? Which adjectives can you use to describe them?
3. Review the comparative forms of the adjectives in the chapter. Make comparative sentences about the two artworks.
4. Gather the information from items 1, 2 and 3 and write a draft of your text.
5. Ask another pair to read your text and give you feedback. Do the same for them.
6. Rewrite your text considering the feedback you received.
7. Revise your text. Check if it is necessary to cut or add information, or even to correct something.
8. Print the works of art and place the text next to them.
9. Observe your classmates' selection of artworks and their texts. Which texts helped you understand the works of art better? Which pieces are the most interesting?
10. Publish your work on the **Students for PEACE Social Media** <www.studentsforpeace.com.br>, using the tag **art** or others chosen by the students.

Peace talk

Chapters 3 and 4
Art for peace

1 **Look at the pictures. What elements do they have in common?**

____

a

Mais amor por favor, urban intervention by Brazilian visual artist Ygor Marotta

b

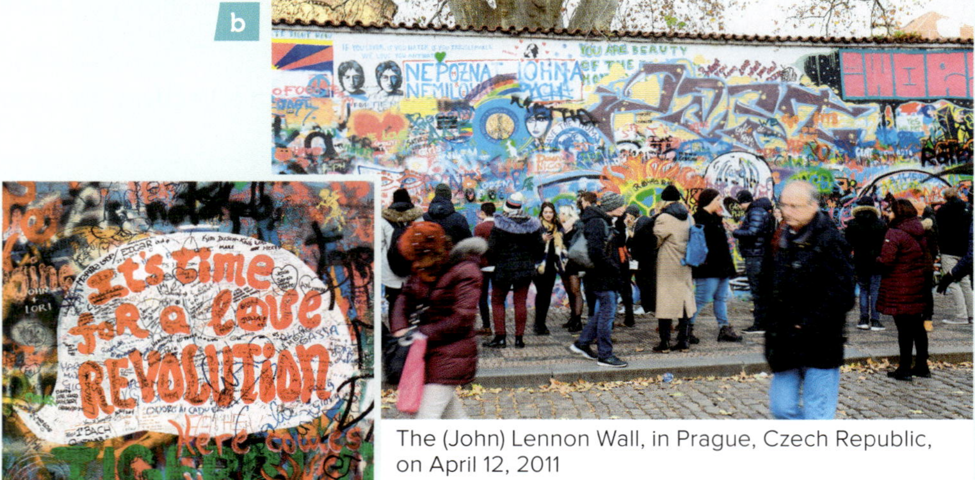

The (John) Lennon Wall, in Prague, Czech Republic, on April 12, 2011

2 **Discuss these questions based on the pictures in activity 1.**

a In your opinion, what motivated Ygor Marotta to create the urban intervention *Mais amor por favor*?

____

b What kind of words or phrases do you think visitors leave on the Lennon Wall?

____

c What do you think of this type of work? Does it really have the power to influence people in a positive way? Explain your answers.

____

3 **Look at this painting. What do you know about it? Use the words in the box to complete a description of this artwork.**

Guernica (1937), by Pablo Picasso. Oil on canvas, 349.3 x 776.6 cm. Museo Reina Sofía, Madrid, Spain

city	Cubist	horrors	planes	symbol	War

Guernica is a painting by ____________ Spanish artist Pablo Picasso. Its name is a reference to the ____________ of Guernica, in Spain, that was heavily bombed by Nazi ____________ on April 26, 1937, during the Spanish Civil ____________.
The painting is an anti-war ____________ to remind people of the ____________ of war.

4 **As a characteristic of the Cubist movement, the images in *Guernica* are not very realistic and things are represented by geometric shapes. Can you find the following elements in the painting? Circle them.**

a Someone looking at the sky with his/her hands reaching up, probably hoping that the destruction stops.

b A white dove (symbol for peace) screaming between two other animals.

c A bull with an expression of shock caused by the horrors surrounding it.

5 **How touched were you by the anti-war message in *Guernica*? Share your feelings with a partner.**

6 **Pablo Picasso painted *Guernica* to protest against the violence of the war. Inspired by that, Kids' Guernica, an international children's art project, has the purpose of expressing the idea of peace and connecting people. In groups, create an artwork to ask for peace. Follow these steps.**

1 Get kraft paper in the size of *Guernica* (3.5 m x 7.8 m) to make a mural.

2 Discuss with your group what "peace" means to you. Then represent it by drawing and painting on the mural.

3 Display your mural at school and, if possible, organize an art exhibition with the other groups.

5 Movie world

1

Alice dreams that she sees the White Rabbit and follows him down the Rabbit-hole, into the Hall of Many Doors.

Alice in Wonderland, a 1903 British silent movie, famous for being the first movie adaptation of Lewis Carroll's book *Alice's Adventures in Wonderland*

4

TOY STORY
TOM HANKS TIM ALLEN
TOY STORY 2
TOY STORY 3
TOY STORY 4

Goals

- Give an oral opinion about your favorite movie.
- Participate in an oral discussion about movie preferences.
- Reflect on the role of movies as a way to raise awareness about a cause.
- Understand and use vocabulary related to movie genres.
- Understand the main ideas of a movie synopsis and its reviews.
- Understand the superlative form of the adjectives when giving opinions about movies.
- Write a movie review.

Spark

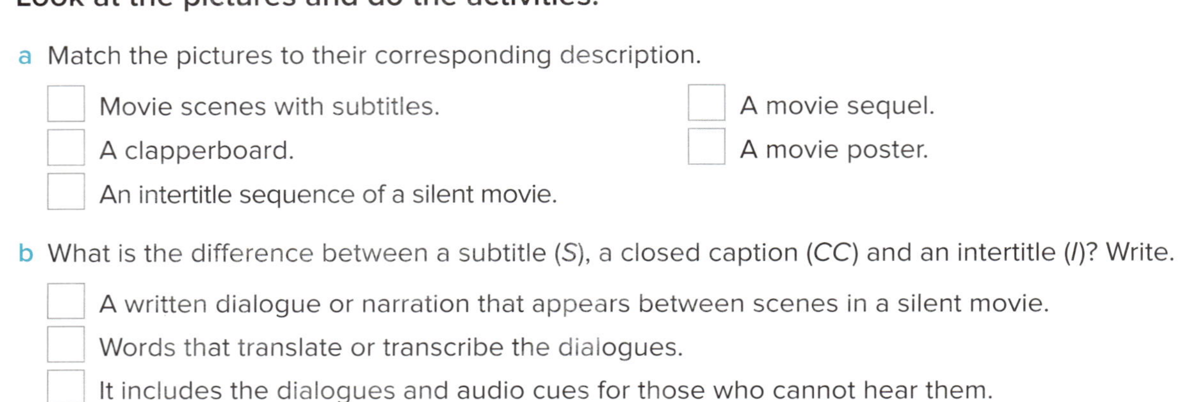

1 Look at the pictures and do the activities.

a Match the pictures to their corresponding description.

- [ ] Movie scenes with subtitles.
- [ ] A clapperboard.
- [ ] An intertitle sequence of a silent movie.
- [ ] A movie sequel.
- [ ] A movie poster.

b What is the difference between a subtitle (*S*), a closed caption (*CC*) and an intertitle (*I*)? Write.

- [ ] A written dialogue or narration that appears between scenes in a silent movie.
- [ ] Words that translate or transcribe the dialogues.
- [ ] It includes the dialogues and audio cues for those who cannot hear them.

2

3

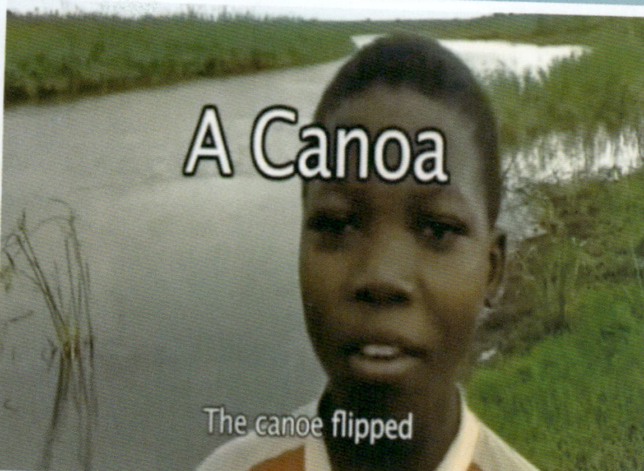

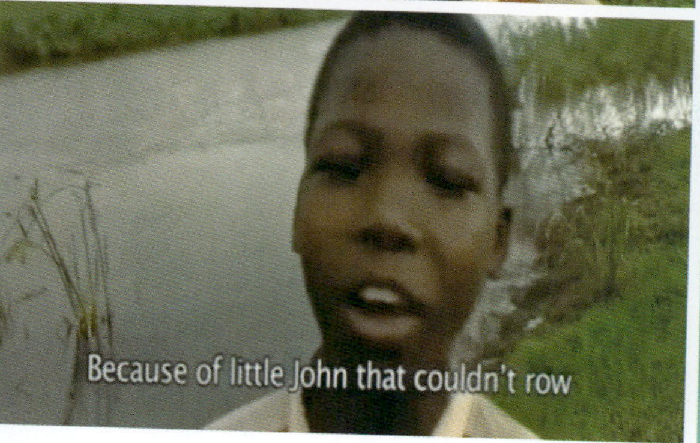

Sequences from a one-minute video produced by children from Chibuto, Mozambique, for *The One Minutes Jr.* initiative, supported by Unicef

5

c Look at the pictures again. Write *T* (true) or *F* (false).

- [ ] Pictures 2 and 4 show big productions.
- [ ] Picture 2 is from a silent movie.
- [ ] Picture 3 shows a documentary project supported by an international organization.
- [ ] Picture 4 is an animation.

Watch:
Silent films

d The movie showed in picture 3 was produced in Mozambique, where Portuguese is spoken as a second language. Why do you think the subtitles are in English?

____

____

____

Explore Movie synopsis and review

Pre-reading

1 Look at texts 1 and 2 and answer the questions. Then share your answers with your classmates.

What kinds of text are these? What is their objective? Circle the appropriate options.

a Text 1 is a movie synopsis/review.

b Text 2 shows movie synopsis/reviews.

c The objective of a movie synopsis/review is to give a critical evaluation of a movie.

d The objective of a movie synopsis/review is to give a brief description of the relevant information about a movie.

Text 1

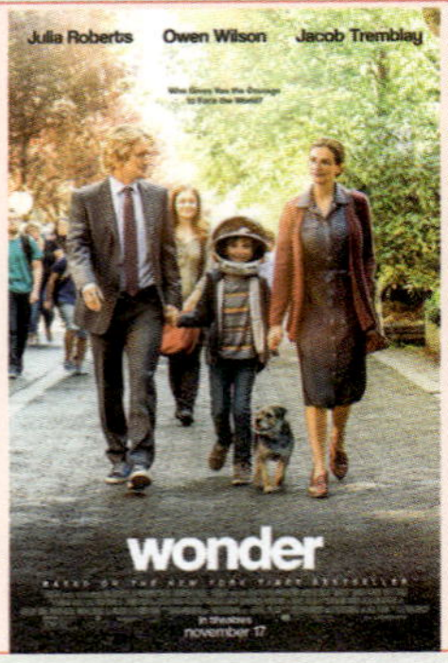

Julia Roberts Owen Wilson Jacob Tremblay

wonder

TOMATOMETER

All Critics | Top Critics

CERTIFIED FRESH Rotten Tomatoes **84%**

Average Rating: 7/10
Reviews Counted: 178
Fresh: 150
Rotten: 28

Critics Consensus: *Wonder* doesn't shy away from its bestselling source material's sentiment, but this well-acted and overall winsome drama earns its tugs at the heartstrings.

AUDIENCE SCORE

88% **liked it**

Average Rating: 4.2/5
User Ratings: 18,513

MOVIE INFO

Based on the *New York Times* bestseller, *WONDER* tells the inspiring and heartwarming story of August Pullman. Born with facial differences that, up until now, have prevented him from going to a mainstream school, Auggie becomes the most unlikely of heroes when he enters the local fifth grade. As his family, his new classmates and the larger community all struggle to find their compassion and acceptance, Auggie's extraordinary journey will unite them all and prove you can't blend in when you were born to stand out.

Rating: PG (parental guidance suggested because some material may not be adequate for young children)
Genre: Drama
Directed by: Stephen Chbosky
Written by: Jack Thorne, Steven Conrad, Stephen Chbosky
In Theaters: Nov 17, 2017 Wide
On Disc/Streaming: Feb 13, 2018
Box Office: $132,090,170
Runtime: 113 minutes
Studio: Lionsgate

Adapted from <https://www.rottentomatoes.com/m/wonder>. Accessed on May 29, 2019.

Text 2

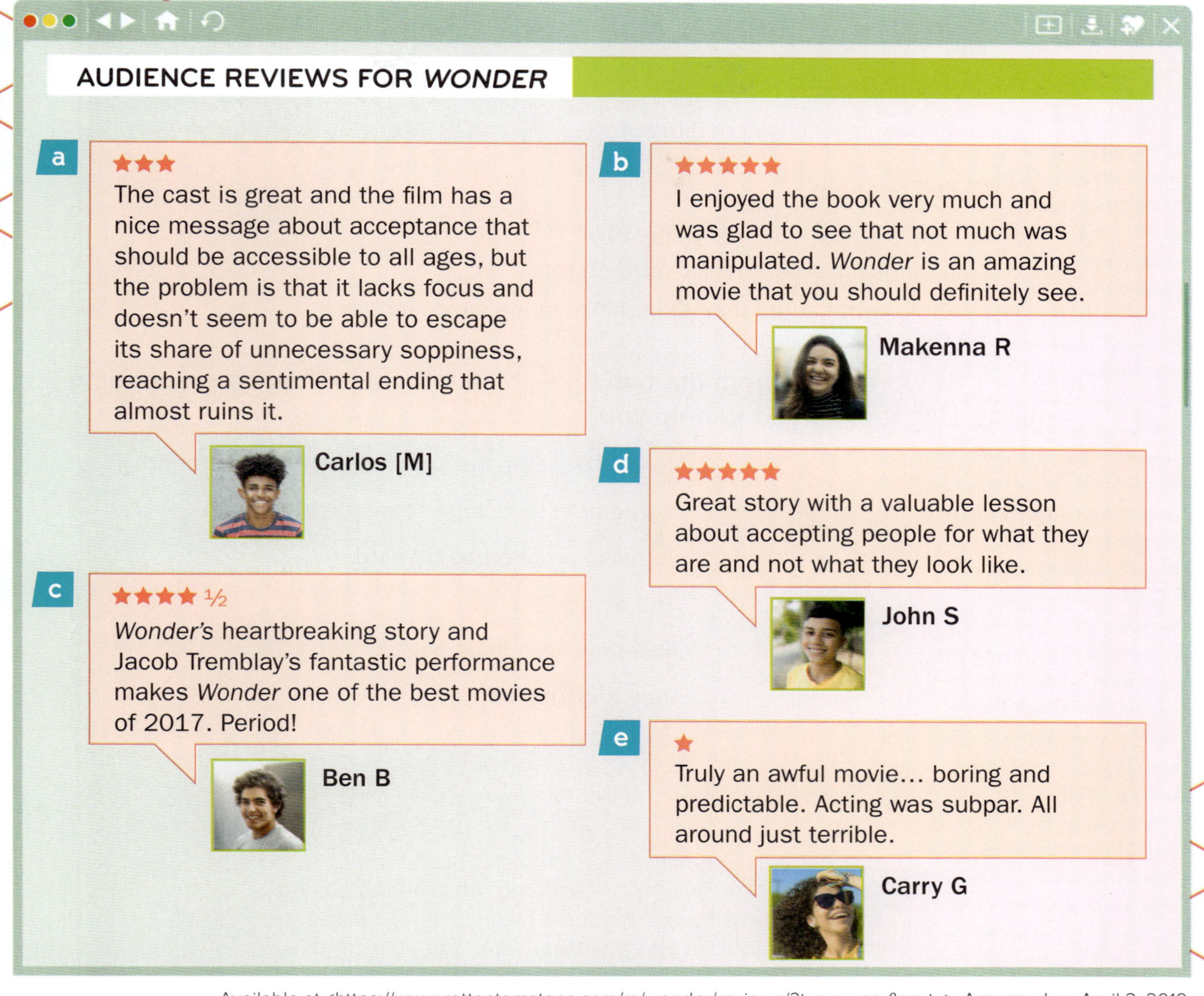

AUDIENCE REVIEWS FOR *WONDER*

a ★★★
The cast is great and the film has a nice message about acceptance that should be accessible to all ages, but the problem is that it lacks focus and doesn't seem to be able to escape its share of unnecessary soppiness, reaching a sentimental ending that almost ruins it.
Carlos [M]

b ★★★★★
I enjoyed the book very much and was glad to see that not much was manipulated. *Wonder* is an amazing movie that you should definitely see.
Makenna R

c ★★★★ ½
Wonder's heartbreaking story and Jacob Tremblay's fantastic performance makes *Wonder* one of the best movies of 2017. Period!
Ben B

d ★★★★★
Great story with a valuable lesson about accepting people for what they are and not what they look like.
John S

e ★
Truly an awful movie... boring and predictable. Acting was subpar. All around just terrible.
Carry G

Available at <https://www.rottentomatoes.com/m/wonder/reviews/?type=user&sort=>. Accessed on April 2, 2019.

Reading

2 **Read text 1 and check the appropriate options.**

a What movie genre is *Wonder*?

- [ ] It's a comedy.
- [ ] It's a drama.

b *Wonder* is...

- [ ] a movie based on a best-seller.
- [ ] an original movie.

c The movie...

- [ ] is recommended for all ages.
- [ ] is not recommended for young children.

3 **Read the reviews from text 2. Then check the appropriate options.**

a The reviews were written by...

- [ ] professional critics.
- [ ] ordinary people who watched the movie.

b How do you know that?

- [ ] The title of the text says "audience reviews".
- [ ] The language includes specific movie terms.
- [ ] The people wrote about their experience in the movie industry.

4 **These words were taken from the two texts. Match them to their corresponding meanings. Use the context to help you.**

a acceptance (*n.*)	[ ] To look or seem the same as the people around.
b awful (*adj.*)	[ ] Agreement to include someone in a group.
c blend in (*v.*)	[ ] To make an effort, to try hard.
d cast (*n.*)	[ ] The actors in a movie.
e soppiness (*n.*)	[ ] Excessively sentimental.
f struggle (*v.*)	[ ] Very bad, unpleasant.

Language clue

In Chapter 2 you worked with suffixes. Texts 1 and 2 use suffixes to identify the word class. The suffix *-ing* in "inspiring", "heartwarming", "amazing" and "heartbreaking" form adjectives that cause some feeling. Other suffixes that generally form adjectives are *-able* and *-ible*, as in "predictable", "valuable", "accessible" and "terrible".

Post-reading

5 **Discuss the questions with your classmates.**

a In texts 1 and 2, there is an example of a movie based on a book. Can you name other movies based on books?

____

b Have you ever seen a movie after reading its book or vice versa? Which one/s? Which version did you prefer?

____

c Have you ever posted a review about a movie on a website like Rotten Tomatoes? What did you think of it?

____

Toolbox Superlative adjectives

1 **Look at the cover of the book *Wonder* and the poster of the movie based on it and read two other reviews for the same movie. Then answer the questions.**

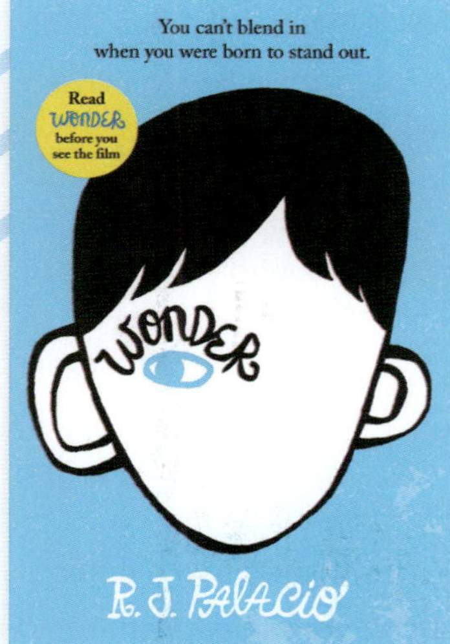

Text 1

Boring! Even my young son said the book was much more interesting than the movie. I wouldn't recommend this snoozer.

Chris F

Text 2

This is one of the most uplifting movies I've ever seen.

Anthony W

Available at <https://www.rottentomatoes.com/m/wonder/reviews/?type=user&sort=r>. Accessed on April 2, 2019.

a What are the adjectives used in the two texts?

____

b Which adjective is being used to compare two elements? What are these two elements?

- [ ] The adjective "interesting". The two elements are the book and the movie.
- [ ] The adjective "uplifting". The two elements are two different movies.

c Which adjective is being used to compare one element to a group of elements? What are these elements?

- [ ] The adjective "interesting". The elements are the book and boring movies.
- [ ] The adjective "uplifting". The elements are the movie *Wonder* and all the other movies that the person has ever seen.

d Which text presents an example of comparison between two elements? Write the sentence.

____

2 Look at these reviews about another movie. Focus on the highlighted words and check the appropriate options.

I "*The Wind Will Carry Us*, a movie by Iranian filmmaker Abbas Kiarostami, is one of the greatest films ever made."

II "How could a film be virtually about nothing and yet manage to speak so profoundly about everything that encompasses life and human existence? It's this enigma that makes *The Wind Will Carry Us* one of the most profoundly hypnotic cinematic experiences of all time."

Adapted from <https://www.thecinemaholic.com/best-iranian-movies/>. Accessed on April 2, 2019.

a The highlighted parts in the reviews are examples of...

- [ ] the comparative form of adjectives, because it compares two elements.
- [ ] the superlative form of adjectives, because it compares one element to a group of elements.

b For short adjectives, like "great", the superlative is formed by...

- [ ] "the" + short adjective + "-est".
- [ ] short adjective + "-est".

c For long adjectives, like "hypnotic", the superlative is formed by...

- [ ] "most" + long adjective.
- [ ] "the most" + long adjective.

Language clue

Just like the comparatives we saw in Chapter 4, there are irregular forms of the superlatives.

Adjective	Comparative form	Superlative form
good	better than	the best
bad	worse than	the worst
far	farther/further than	the farthest/furthest

3 Now, talk to a partner and express your opinion using these structures.

- The greatest actor/actress is ____________________.
- The most creative director is ____________________.
- The least interesting movie genre is ____________________.
- The most hilarious movie is ____________________.
- The best movie ever made is ____________________.
- The worst movie ever made is ____________________.

Building blocks Movie genres

1 **Talk to a partner and answer the questions.**

a Look back at text 1 in the "Explore" section. What movie genre is *Wonder*?

____

b What are the characteristics of this genre?

- [ ] It tends to be more serious and involves conflicts and emotions.
- [ ] It intends to make the audience laugh and sometimes uses jokes or satirical sketches.
- [ ] It deals with concepts such as science and technology, space exploration, time travel and extraterrestrial life.

c What are your favorite and least favorite movie genres?

____

2 **Look and label the movie scenes using the genres from the box.**

adventure animation comedy documentary fantasy horror musical romance sci-fi (science fiction) thriller

3 **Now, use some of the words from activity 2 to complete the following definitions.**

a ______________________ movies are often related to scientific and technological development, involving heroes, aliens, distant planets, travels and creatures from space.

b ______________________ movies are usually exciting stories, with new experiences or exotic places, very similar to the "action movie" genre.

c ______________________ movies are entertaining plots deliberately designed to make people laugh.

d ______________________ movies are developed around stories involving a lot of suspense.

e ______________________ movies are love stories that focus on passion, emotion and the romantic involvement between the characters.

f ______________________ movies are made with computer-generated images.

g ______________________ movies provide factual records or reports of something from the real world.

h ______________________ movies are stories created in order to generate strong reactions, such as fear or surprise.

4 **Two movie genres from activity 2 were not included in activity 3. Work with a partner and write your own definitions for them.**

____

____

____

5 **Let's play a game! In pairs, describe a movie genre and let your partner guess it. Then change roles.**

It usually involves science and technology. Sometimes there are alien creatures, remote planets etc.

It's sci-fi!

Sync Listening: Teen talk

Pre-listening

1 **You are going to listen to some teenagers talking about their favorite movies and movie series. Which of these adjectives do you think you will hear?**

a ☐ amazing
b ☐ boring
c ☐ classic
d ☐ delicious
e ☐ entertaining
f ☐ funny
g ☐ impossible
h ☐ the best

Listening

2 10 **Listen to the audio to check your predictions from activity 1. Then listen again and check the titles of movies and movie series that are mentioned.**

a ☐ *Horton Hears a Who!*
b ☐ *Driving Miss Daisy*
c ☐ *Harry Potter*
d ☐ *Jurassic World*
e ☐ *The Lion King*
f ☐ *Napoleon Dynamite*
g ☐ *Star Trek*
h ☐ *Star Wars*

3 10 **Listen again and answer the questions.**

a What is the name of the program?

____

b What kind of students participate in the program: elementary, high school or college students?

____

c What is the first question that the hostess asks: about favorite movies or about favorite movie series?

____

4 10 **Listen again and match the movies to the phrases that describe them.**

a *Driving Miss Daisy* ☐ A classic, funny movie.
b *Napoleon Dynamite* ☐ A big part of his childhood.
c *The Lion King* ☐ The storyline is amazing and it has a lot of meaning.

Post-listening

5 **Discuss these questions with the whole class.**

a Are the teenagers interviewed boys or girls?

b Is there a stereotyped way of thinking? Do you believe some movies are more for boys than for girls?

Sync Speaking: Discussion: favorite movies

Pre-speaking

1 Answer the questions. Then share your answers with a partner.

a What is/are your favorite movie genre/s?

____

b What is your favorite movie?

____

c Why do you like it?

____

d What adjectives can you use to describe your favorite movie?

____

e Who are the main actors?

____

f When did you watch it for the first time?

____

g How many times have you seen it?

____

Speaking

2 Form a circle with your classmates. Follow the instructions.

a Share your answers to the questions in activity 1 with your classmates.

b Make comments when other people present their favorite movies.

c If you need to interrupt someone, be respectful.

Post-speaking

3 Talk about your oral production in activity 2. Discuss the following questions.

a How would you evaluate your presentation? Was it clear?

b Did you interrupt anyone or were you interrupted while speaking? If so, was it done in a respectful way?

Studio Movie review

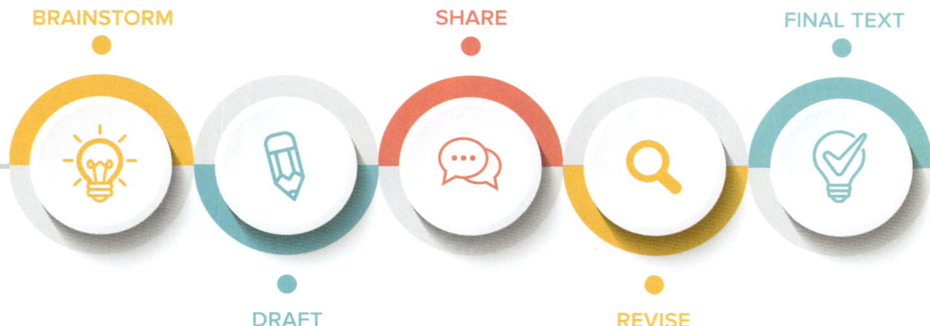

What: a movie review
To whom: for personal use; other students
Media: paper; digital
Objective: write a short review of a movie

1. Choose a movie. Make a list of what you can say about it.
2. Write a summary with its main ideas.
3. Rewrite your notes in a paragraph. Use the words "because", "but", "so" etc. to connect your ideas.
4. After finishing your first draft, check if it is clear and well-structured.
5. Share your text with a partner. Ask for feedback.
6. Revise your text according to the feedback received.
7. Choose a picture to illustrate your text. Don't forget to write down its source.
8. Share your movie review with your classmates. See if any text grabs your attention.
9. Publish your work on the **Students for PEACE Social Media** <www.studentsforpeace.com.br>, using the tags **reviews, moviereviews, movies** or others chosen by the students.

6 From cover to cover

1

2

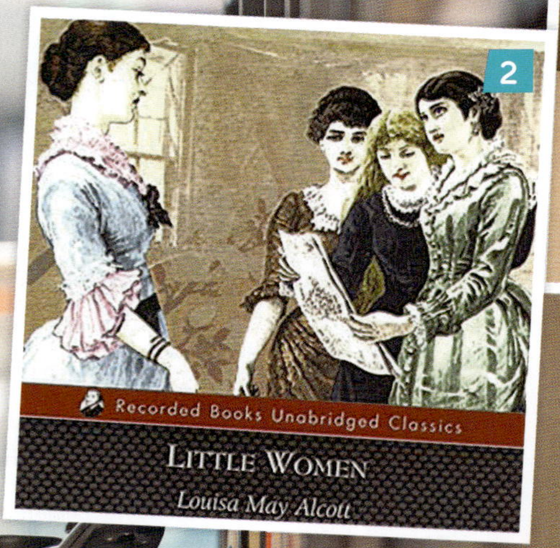

Recorded Books Unabridged Classics

LITTLE WOMEN

Louisa May Alcott

Goals

- Express preferences about reading.
- Identify some of the main literary genres.
- Make a summary of a literary piece for an oral presentation.
- Read and explore excerpts from literary pieces.
- Review the uses of the past simple and the past continuous.
- Understand an oral summary of a literary piece.
- Write a piece of short fiction (microfiction).

1 What does each picture show? Check the appropriate descriptions.

- [ ] A person in a library.
- [ ] A bookstore.
- [ ] An audiobook cover (*Little Women*).
- [ ] *Cordel* literature.
- [ ] Comic books.
- [ ] Hardcover books and an e-book.
- [ ] A cover from a juvenile novel (*Charlie and the Chocolate Factory*).
- [ ] Children coloring books.

2 Do you generally go to libraries? What can you find there?

____

____

3 What do you know about the kind of literature in picture 5? Circle the appropriate words to complete the definition.

Cordel literature (from the Portuguese term *literatura de cordel*, literally "string literature") are popular and **expensively/inexpensively** printed booklets or pamphlets containing **folk/love** novels, poems and **songs/documentaries**, which are produced and sold by **librarians/vendors** in big **bookstores/fairs** in the **Northeast/South** of Brazil. Its name comes from the fact that the booklets are usually hung on a **wall/string** for sale.

Adapted from <https://en.wikipedia.org/wiki/Cordel_literature>. Accessed on April 4, 2019.

L1

Explore A classic of literature

Pre-reading

1 **Look at the pictures and read some information about this book. Then write *Yes* or *No*.**

Author: Mary Shelley
Country: United Kingdom
Language: English
Genre: Gothic novel, horror fiction, science-fiction
Published: January 1, 1818

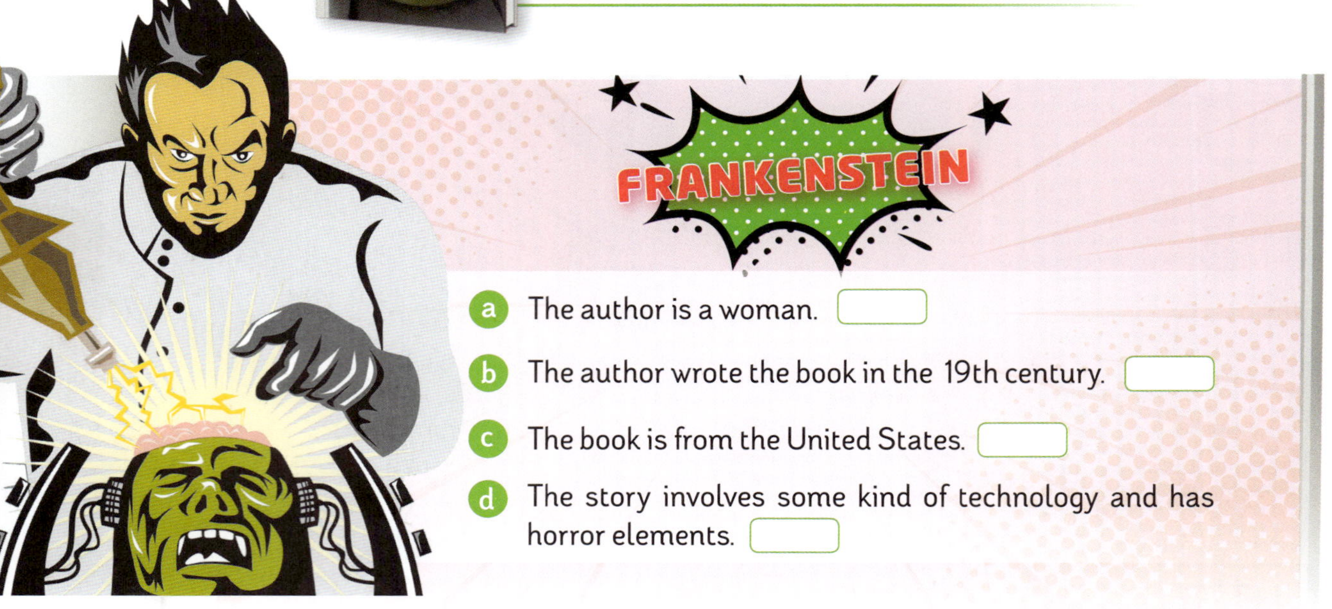

a) The author is a woman. ______

b) The author wrote the book in the 19th century. ______

c) The book is from the United States. ______

d) The story involves some kind of technology and has horror elements. ______

Going further

What do you know about *Frankenstein*? If you don't know anything about it, do some research and share your findings with your classmates.

Reading

2 **Read the following excerpt from *Frankenstein* and order the events (1-4).**

a [ ] The scientist had difficulty to relax and sleep that night.
b [ ] The creature's arms, legs and other body parts were in harmony with one another.
c [ ] The creature made its first body movements.
d [ ] The scientist mentions how much time he spent working to create a living creature.

Text 1

CHAPTER 5 (*EXCERPT*)

It was on a dreary night of November that I beheld my accomplishment. With an anxiety that felt like agony, I collected the instruments of life around me to infuse a spark of being into the lifeless thing that lay at my feet. It was already one in the morning; when I saw the dull yellow eye of the creature open, it breathed hard, and a convulsive motion agitated its limbs.

How can I describe my emotions at this creation? His limbs were in proportion, and I had selected his beautiful features. Oh, God!

The different accidents of life are not so changeable as the feelings of human nature. I had worked hard for nearly two years, for the sole purpose of infusing life into an inanimate body. For this I had deprived myself of rest and health. I had desired it with an ardour that far exceeded moderation; but now that I had finished, the beauty of the dream vanished, and horror and disgust filled my heart. Unable to face the being I had created, I rushed out of the room and continued a long time traversing my bedchamber, unable to sleep.

Adapted from SHELLEY, Mary W. ***Frankenstein;* or, The Modern Prometheus.** Project Gutenberg, 2008.

3 **Read the excerpt again and check the appropriate sentences about the story.**

a ☐ The scientist himself tells the story.

b ☐ The story is told by a third person.

c ☐ The scientist was pleased with his creation because it was alive.

d ☐ The scientist did not like the creature he created.

4 **Read other excerpts from *Frankenstein* and answer the questions.**

I And what was I? Of my creation and creator I was absolutely ignorant, but I knew that I possessed no money, no friends, no kind of property. I was, besides, endued with a figure hideously deformed and loathsome; I was not even of the same nature as man. When I looked around I saw and heard of none like me. Was I, then, a monster? **Chapter 13** (excerpt)

II Hateful day when I received life! Accursed creator! Why did you form a monster so hideous that even *you* turned from me in disgust? **Chapter 15** (excerpt)

III This was then the reward of my benevolence! I had saved a human being from destruction, and as a recompense I now suffered the miserable pain of a wound which shattered the flesh and bone. Inflamed by pain, I vowed eternal hatred and vengeance to all mankind! **Chapter 16** (excerpt)

IV We may not part until you have promised to fulfill my request. I am alone and miserable, but one as deformed and horrible as myself would not deny herself to me. My companion must be of the same species and have the same defects. **Chapter 16** (excerpt)

Adapted from: SHELLEY, Mary W. ***Frankenstein;* or, The Modern Prometheus.** Project Gutenberg, 2008.

a Who said the words in these excerpts? Show evidence in the text.

☐ The scientist. ☐ The creature.

b Write the number of the excerpt that shows that the creature...

☐ was born innocent, but became a monster that hated all humans because he was abandoned and unloved.

☐ knows he is going to be alone because of his appearance.

☐ knows his creator did not like him.

☐ wants to have someone to keep him company.

5 **What do the words in bold mean? Match each item to its corresponding definition. Go back to text 1 and activity 4 to see these words highlighted in context.**

a ☐ "on a **dreary** night"
b ☐ "I **beheld** my accomplishment"
c ☐ "I saw the **dull** yellow eye"
d ☐ "the beauty of my dreams **vanished**"
e ☐ "a figure **hideously** deformed"
f ☐ "a monster so **hideous**"

I *adjective:* colorless, lightless
II *adjective:* repulsive, grotesque
III *verb:* to contemplate, to see, to observe
IV *verb:* to disappear suddenly and completely
V *adverb:* repulsively, grotesquely
VI *adjective:* depressing, sad

Going further

Do you know what happens next in *Frankenstein*? Do you have the book? If not, the story is available online. Explore "Project Gutenberg" (https://www.gutenberg.org/) to find this and other literary classics.

Going further

Frankenstein; or, The Modern Prometheus was written by British author Mary Shelley when she was only 19. It is considered one of the first sci-fi books ever.

Post-reading

6 **Discuss these questions with your classmates. Then check.**

a In your opinion, who made the worst mistake?

☐ The scientist, who abandoned his creature.
☐ The creature, who became cruel to others as a revenge against his creator and all who hurt him.

b How does this story compare to making a clone? Check the alternative that best describes your opinion.

☐ Making a clone is unethical because it is like creating another creature.
☐ It's OK if the person accepts to be cloned.
☐ It's unethical because it interferes in nature.
☐ It's ethical if you do it for a good reason, such as helping to stop a disease.
☐ Other: ____________________

Toolbox Past simple x Past continuous (review)

1 **Read these sentences from the excerpts in the "Explore" section and answer the question: in what verb tense are they?**

a "It was on a dreary night of November [...]."

b "His limbs were in proportion [...]."

c "And what was I?"

d "I was not even of the same nature as man."

e "When I looked around I saw and heard of none like me. Was I, then, a monster?"

f "Why did you form a monster so hideous that even you turned from me in disgust?"

____

2 **Read the sentences in activity 1 again and use the verbs to complete the charts.**

Past simple (regular verbs)	Past simple (irregular verbs)	Past simple (auxiliary verb)

3 **Now write the verbs from activity 2 next to their corresponding form.**

a do: ____________

b to be: ____________

c to hear: ____________

d to look: ____________

e to see: ____________

f to turn: ____________

4 **Read the sentences from activity 1 again and complete the statements. Use the words from the box.**

did	infinitive	irregular verbs	not	was	were

a In affirmative sentences with the verb *to be* in the past simple, we use ________________ when the subject is *I/he/she/it* (or equivalent) and ________________ when the subject is *you/we/they* (or equivalent).

b In negative sentences with the verb *to be* in the past simple, we use the past form of the verb *to be* + ________________.

c To form questions in the past simple, we invert the positions of the subject and the verb *to be* or we use the auxiliary verb ________________ before a pronoun or a noun.

d In questions in the past simple, the main verb is in the ________________.

e The verbs that do not end in *ed* in the past simple are called ________________.

Language clue

To put most regular verbs into the past simple, add *-ed*: look**ed**, turn**ed**, watch**ed**, listen**ed**. However, if the regular verb ends in *e*, just add *-d*: translate**d**, like**d**. And if the regular verb ends in ***y*** next to a consonant, replace ***y*** with ***i*** and add *-ed*: stud**ied**. Irregular verbs don't follow any rules: have → had; think → thought; get → got; be → was/were.

5 **Read these excerpts from other novels and write if the statements are *T* (true) or *F* (false). Then justify your answers.**

Text 1

Zhang Ping and Choy Lee watched the coverage of the crash of Air Force One on a television in Choy's apartment. He had a big flat-screen television made in China.

Zhang's English was improving — he listened very carefully and watched a lot of television — but he had a long way to go, so Choy translated whenever the announcer was saying something that he thought Zhang might like to know.

Adapted from COONTS, Stephen. ***The Art of War:* A Novel.** New York: St. Martin's Press, 2016. p. 110.

Text 2

"I have a little present for you, Rose," said Papa.

He handed me a rectangular package that looked promisingly like a book. I love reading more than anything else, especially the books in Papa's studio.

I opened my package eagerly, though I feared it would be a Mrs. Molesworth or a Miss Yonge, the sort of authors considered suitable for a girl of thirteen.

But it wasn't a novel at all, for children or adults. It was a sketchbook, every page blank.

"I thought this would be a good time for you to start sketching seriously, sweetheart."

I didn't know what to say. He was trying so hard to cheer me up.

Adapted from WILSON, Jacqueline. ***Rose Rivers:* A Victorian Tale from the World of Hetty Feather.** London: Penguin Books, 2018. n.p.

a In text 1...

- [ ] we read the narration of a trip that two people took to China.

____

- [ ] one of the people involved doesn't know the local language well.

____

b In text 2...

- [ ] the story narrated involves a girl and her grandfather.

____

- [ ] we infer that the girl was probably upset or sad before receiving the present.

____

6 Go back to the texts in activity 5 and follow the instructions.

a Underline the verbs in the past simple.

b Circle the verbs in the past continuous.

c Now underline the appropriate options in the following sentences:

I The **past continuous/past simple** is used to narrate an event that has a beginning and an end in the past.

II The **past continuous/past simple** is used to describe an action that was in progress at a certain time in the past.

d Write *A* (affirmative), *N* (negative) or *I* (interrogative) to identify how we form the past continuous.

- [ ] "Was"/"Were" + subject + main verb + *-ing*?
- [ ] Subject + "was"/"were" + "not" + main verb + *-ing*.
- [ ] Subject + "was"/"were" + main verb + *-ing*.

Building blocks Literary genres

1 Look at the book covers. What genre is each one? Use the words in the box to label them.

adventure	fantasy	graphic novel	poetry	romance	sci-fi (science fiction)

a

b
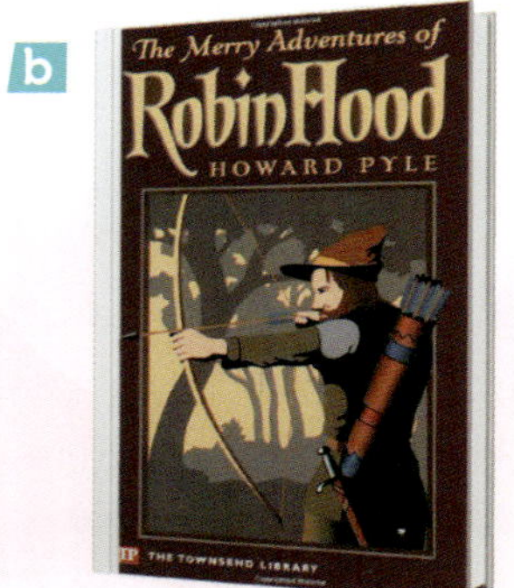

c

d

e

f

2 Match each literary genre (a-f) in activity 1 to its definition.

- [ ] This genre contains words that follow a certain rhythm or structure, and sometimes rhyme, which are created to evoke emotion.
- [ ] Stories of a love relationship.
- [ ] Narratives in which the protagonist goes on an epic journey.
- [ ] Stories that involve technology, computers, machines, traveling through space, time or to other universes.
- [ ] Stories about magic or supernatural forces in invented worlds or in a legendary, mythic past.
- [ ] A novel in comic-strip format that uses lots of pictures, onomatopoeia and speech bubbles.

3 Ask and answer these questions with a partner.

a What is/are your favorite literary genre/s?

b Are you currently reading any book? If so, which one? What genre is it?

Watch:
Writing in English

Portrait of British author Charlotte Brontë (1816-1855)

Sync Listening: A novel summary

Pre-listening

1 **Look at the picture and read its caption. Go to page 80 and look for the same picture. Then circle the appropriate options.**

Charlotte Brontë was a British/Scottish author. She wrote *The Lord of the Rings*/*Jane Eyre*.

Listening

2 11 **Listen to the introduction of the summary of *Jane Eyre*. What is mentioned about Charlotte Brontë's book?**

a ☐ She wrote *Jane Eyre* under a pseudonym of a male author, Currer Bell.
b ☐ She wrote *Jane Eyre* with the help of her friend Currer Bell.

3 12 **Listen to the second part of the audio and check the appropriate answer.**

a How old is Jane when the story begins?
☐ 11 years old. ☐ 10 years old.

b Who does Jane live with as a child?
☐ Her aunt and her cousins. ☐ Her mother and father.

c What type of school does Jane go to?
☐ A public school. ☐ An orphan school.

d What happens to Jane's friend Helen Burns?
☐ She dies. ☐ She moves away.

4 13 **Listen to the third part of the audio and write *T* (true) or *F* (false).**

a ☐ Jane puts out the fire in Mr. Rochester's room and saves his life.
b ☐ Jane goes back to her aunt's because she misses her.
c ☐ When Jane returns, Mr. Rochester reveals to her that he is secretly married.
d ☐ Jane and Mr. Rochester's marriage is interrupted because a lawyer reveals he is already married.

Post-listening

5 **Discuss these questions with your classmates.**

a What adjectives would you use to describe Jane? Check and explain why.

☐ unpredictable ☐ intelligent ☐ strong
☐ sad ☐ revengeful ☐ resilient

b Do you like this kind of story? Why?

Sync Speaking: Summarizing a book

Pre-speaking

1 **Answer the following questions with your classmates.**

a What are your favorite books? Consider books written in any language.

b What helps you choose a book to read?

☐ A synopsis. ☐ A review.
☐ The author. ☐ A summary.

2 **Do you know what a presentation of a book summary is?**

____

____

3 **Present a book summary. Follow the instructions.**

a Work in groups. Each group should choose a book for all the members to read.

b Take note of the book's author, characters, plot, organization etc.

c Set a deadline for all the members to finish reading the book.

d As you read the book, take notes.

e After you have read the book, prepare the text of your book summary. Use the summary presented in the "Sync – Listening" section as a reference. These tips may also be useful:

- Prepare your book summary with the events in chronological order.
- Describe the main points of the story and the main characters.

Speaking

4 **Make an oral presentation of your book summary.**

Useful language

We're/I'm going to talk about...
This book was written by... in...
The main characters are...
The book tells the story of...
The story begins with/when...

Post-speaking

5 **Talk about these questions with your classmates.**

a What was interesting about the books and/or authors presented?

b After listening to all the summaries, which book/s would you like to read? Explain your answer.

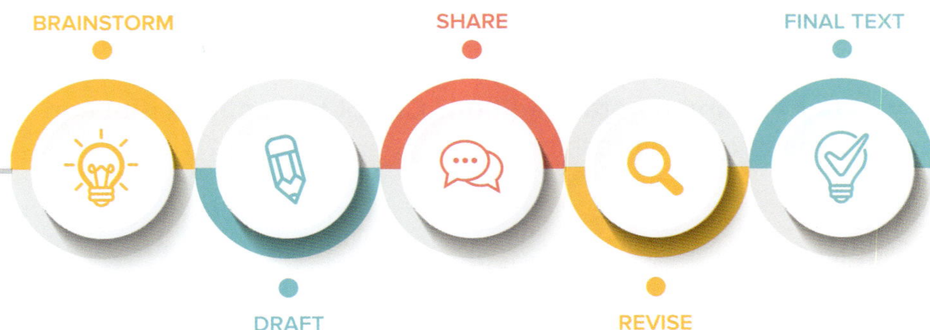

What: a microfiction
To whom: classmates; teacher; general public
Media: paper; digital
Objective: write a fictitious story in 300 words or less

1. What kind of stories do you prefer? Consider the genres you have learned in this chapter. What should you find in these types of stories?
2. Think of a good story and its components. Where does it take place? When? Who is involved? Who are the main characters? What is the plot?
3. Your challenge is to write a 300-word fiction. You may research microfiction techniques to help you out.
4. Write a draft of your story. Don't count the words yet, just focus on the plot using your imagination.
5. Check the previous sections of this chapter for examples of narrative excerpts and make changes in your text if necessary.
6. Share your draft with your classmates. Ask for feedback.
7. Revise your text according to the feedback received and consider the limit of 300 words.
8. Write the final version of your microfiction. Share it with your classmates.
9. Your class could make a booklet of stories to be displayed in the school library. Publish your work on the **Students for PEACE Social Media** <www.studentsforpeace.com.br>, using the tag **microfiction** or others chosen by the students.

Peace talk

Chapters 5 and 6
Safeguarding oral traditions

1 **What do you understand by oral tradition? Check the options that can be considered forms of oral expression.**

____

a ☐ folk tales
b ☐ jokes
c ☐ legends
d ☐ letters
e ☐ manuscripts
f ☐ nursery rhymes
g ☐ proverbs
h ☐ riddles
i ☐ travel diaries

2 **Read this excerpt from a text produced by UNESCO and use it as a reference to check your answers in activity 1.**

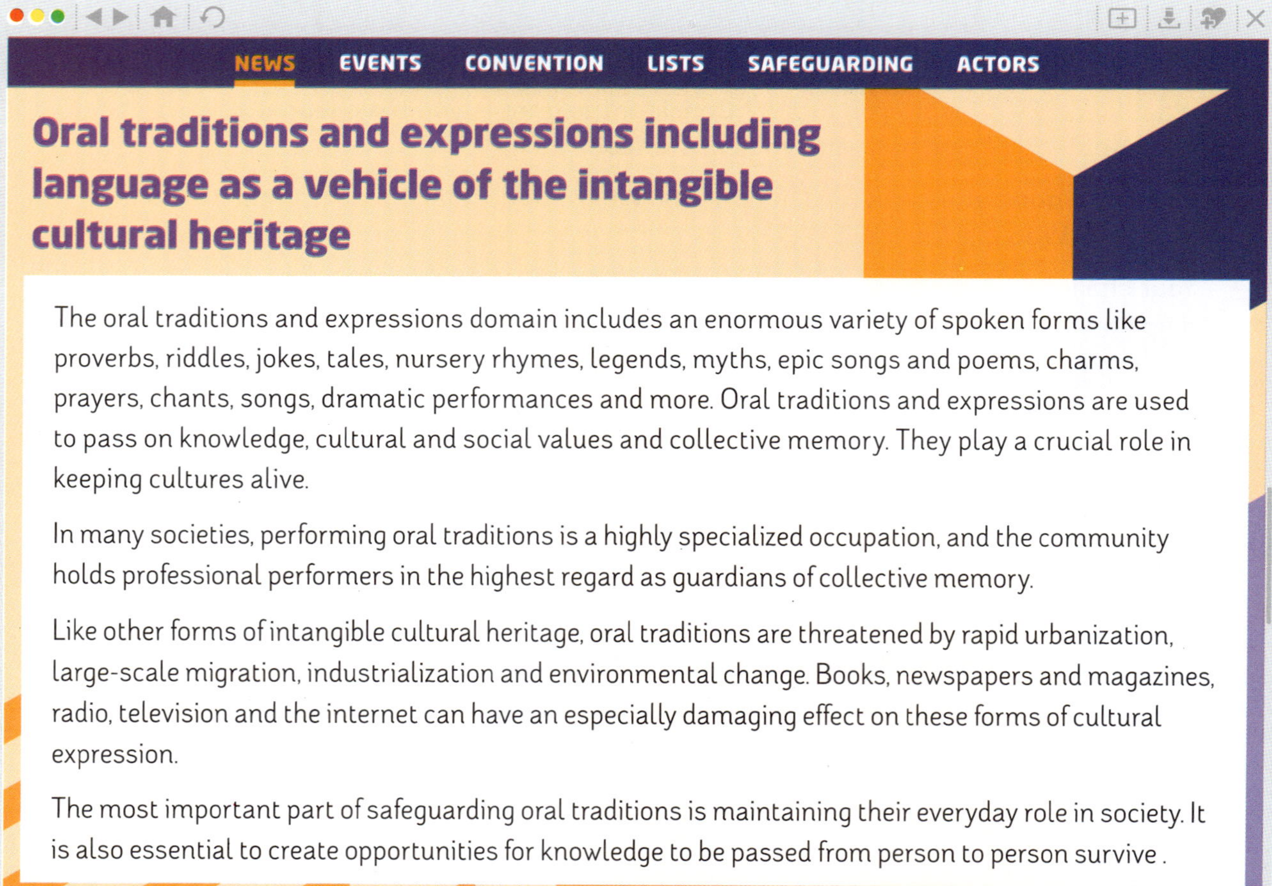

Oral traditions and expressions including language as a vehicle of the intangible cultural heritage

The oral traditions and expressions domain includes an enormous variety of spoken forms like proverbs, riddles, jokes, tales, nursery rhymes, legends, myths, epic songs and poems, charms, prayers, chants, songs, dramatic performances and more. Oral traditions and expressions are used to pass on knowledge, cultural and social values and collective memory. They play a crucial role in keeping cultures alive.

In many societies, performing oral traditions is a highly specialized occupation, and the community holds professional performers in the highest regard as guardians of collective memory.

Like other forms of intangible cultural heritage, oral traditions are threatened by rapid urbanization, large-scale migration, industrialization and environmental change. Books, newspapers and magazines, radio, television and the internet can have an especially damaging effect on these forms of cultural expression.

The most important part of safeguarding oral traditions is maintaining their everyday role in society. It is also essential to create opportunities for knowledge to be passed from person to person survive .

Adapted from <https://ich.unesco.org/en/oral-traditions-and-expressions-00053>. Accessed on September 29, 2018.

3 Answer the questions according to the excerpt in activity 2.

a What is the importance of oral traditions?

b What examples of modern media can have a damaging effect on oral traditions? How do you think these media can harm this form of cultural expression?

c How can we protect oral traditions?

4 Look at these pictures and talk to a partner about the questions.

a What do the pictures represent?

b Did you use to have this kind of interaction with the elderly when you were a child? If so, were you a good listener?

c What kind of knowledge can the elderly pass on to the young that cannot be found in books?

5 Have a round-table discussion on safeguarding oral traditions. Follow the instructions.

1 Research stories, superstitions, proverbs and other oral expressions that your grandparents and great-grandparents used to have/use. Try to find out how they learned them.

2 Organize the information you collected and take notes on your impressions about them.

3 Organize the round-table discussion. Decide the order of the speakers and the moment when the audience can interrupt them for comments or questions.

7 Communication

Goals

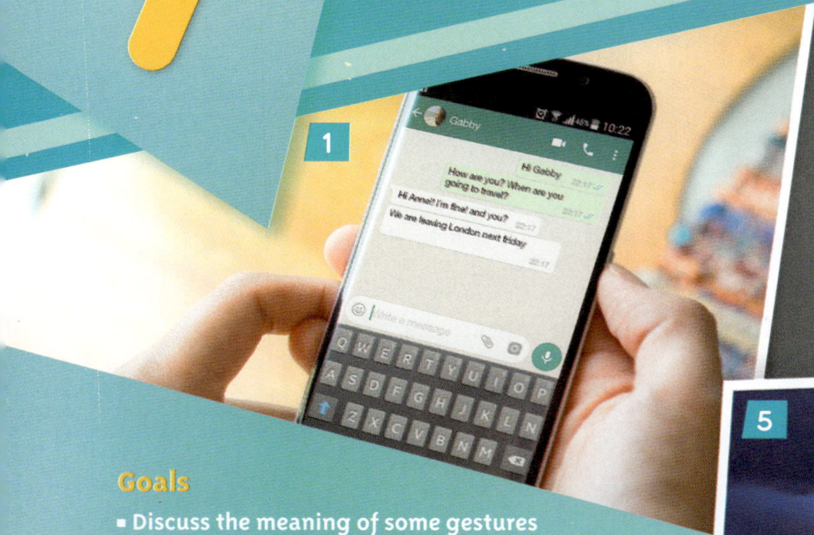

- Discuss the meaning of some gestures and expressions in different cultures.
- Identify different means of communication and think about their pros and cons.
- Make predictions about the future of communication.
- Recognize and use the future tense with "will" and "going to".
- Recognize the characteristics of "notes" and "letters".
- Write a letter telling someone about your future plans and dreams and asking about this person's plans and dreams.

Discuss these questions with your classmates.

a Look at the pictures. What do they have in common?

____

____

b Which of these items do you use the most? Why?

- [ ] texting
- [ ] post-it messages
- [ ] face-to-face conversation
- [ ] other: ____________

c Pictures 3, 4 and 5 show forms of non-verbal communication. Why are they used? Write the numbers in the boxes according to the pictures.

- [ ] To give instructions for pedestrians.
- [ ] To orientate maritime pilots at sea or on inland waterways.
- [ ] To indicate the preferential or exclusive use of cyclists.

d Which means of communication used to be popular in the past? What about nowadays?

____

____

Explore Notes and letters

Pre-reading

1 **Look at the pictures. Then discuss these questions with your classmates.**

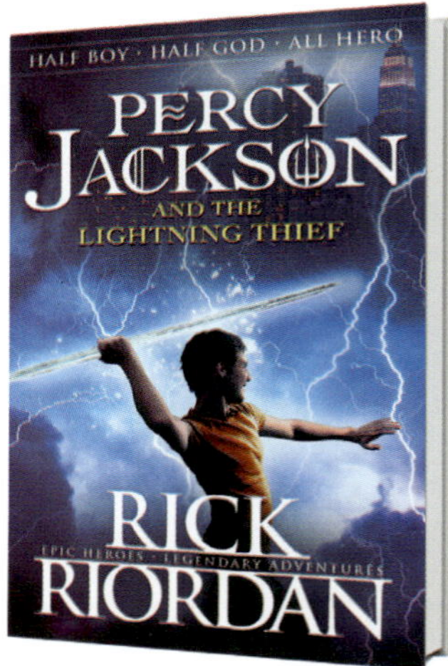

a Have you read either of these books or seen any of the movies based on them? Do you know anything about their stories and characters?

b In activities 2 and 4 you are going to read a note from a book of the *Percy Jackson* series and a letter from a book of the series *The Lord of the Rings*. Have you ever written or received a note or a letter?

Reading

2 **Read this note. Then check the appropriate sentences.**

Dear Grover,
Woods outside Toronto attacked by giant evil badger. Tried to do as you suggested and summon power of Pan. No effect. Many naiads' trees destroyed. Retreating to Ottawa. Please advise. Where are you?

Gleeson
Hedge,
protector

RIORDAN, Rick. ***Percy Jackson & the Olympians: The Last Olympian***. London: Puffin, 2009. p. 65.

a ☐ It mentions mostly past events.
b ☐ It mentions mostly future events.
c ☐ It expects some kind of reaction and response from the receiver.
d ☐ It presents short and reduced sentences.
e ☐ It mentions the names of the sender and receiver.
f ☐ Its message is not urgent.
g ☐ Its writer needs some help about what to do.

3 Read the text again and check the appropriate answers.

a According to the note, it is possible to say that it is probably about...

- [ ] a war.
- [ ] good news.

b Who sends and who receives the note?

- [ ] Grover sends a note to Gleeson.
- [ ] Gleeson sends a note to Grover.

c What does the sender of the note want to know from the person who receives it?

- [ ] His location and advice.
- [ ] More about the situation in the woods.

4 Now read this letter from the series *The Lord of the Rings* and match the numbers to the parts of the letter they indicate. Work with a partner.

1 THE PRANCING PONY, BREE. Midyear's Day, Shire Year, 1418.

2 Dear Frodo,

3 Bad news has reached me here. I must go off at once. You had better leave Bag End soon, and get out of the Shire before the end of July at latest. I will return as soon as I can; and I will follow you, if I find that you are gone. Leave a message for me here, if you pass through Bree. You can trust the landlord (Butterbur). You may meet a friend of mine on the Road: a Man, lean, dark, tall, by some called Strider. He knows our business and will help you. Make for Rivendell. There I hope we may meet again. If I do not come, Elrond will advise you.

4 Yours in haste,

5 GANDALF

6 PS. Do NOT use It again, not for any reason whatever! Do not travel by night!

PPS. Make sure that it is the real Strider. There are many strange men on the roads. His true name is Aragorn.

TOLKIEN, John R. R. ***The Lord of the Rings:* The Fellowship of the Ring**. London: HarperCollins Publishers, 2008. p. 222.

a [ ] Postscript: the part where you write your final notes (after signing the letter).

b [ ] Signature: where you put your name.

c [ ] Heading: it includes the address and the date.

d [ ] Greeting: the salutation.

e [ ] Closing: a short capitalized expression, such as "Love," "Best wishes" or "Sincerely".

f [ ] Body: where you write the message that you need to deliver.

5 **Read the letter from activity 4 again. Then check the appropriate options.**

a According to the letter, Gandalf is going to...

- [ ] leave the place where he is immediately.
- [ ] wait for some weeks before he leaves the place where he is.
- [ ] stay where he is and wait for Frodo's visit.

b Gandalf tells Frodo to...

- [ ] use the magic ring again if he needs to.
- [ ] stay where he is and wait for Gandalf.
- [ ] leave the place where he is.

c What does Gandalf mention about Strider?

- [ ] He mentions that there are lots of real men named Strider.
- [ ] He mentions that Aragorn is his real name.
- [ ] He mentions that Frodo must be careful when meeting him.

6 **Think about notes and letters in general and their characteristics. Now write *N* (note) or *L* (letter).**

a [ ] It is concise and focuses on a short and objective message.
b [ ] It may be short or long.
c [ ] It may present different subjects.
d [ ] It is usually sent by mail.
e [ ] It usually indicates the place where the sender is and the date.
f [ ] It is usually left in a specific place or delivered in person.

Post-reading

7 **Discuss these questions with your classmates.**

a In your opinion, could the note in activity 2 have been sent via text message or audio message, considering the context of the story? Why?

____

____

b In the past, messages like letters and notes used to take several days or even months to get to their destination. How would you feel if you no longer had modern technology to send messages?

____

____

c If you have never written a letter, would you like to write one? Why?

____

____

Toolbox "Will" x "going to"

1 **Read the excerpts taken from the letter in the "Explore" section and circle the appropriate options.**

"I will return as soon as I can; and I will follow you, if I find that you are gone."

a It is possible to say that Gandalf **knows exactly when/doesn't know when** he is going to come back.

b In this excerpt, it is possible to say that Gandalf **knows exactly where Frodo will be (he is certain of that)/doesn't know if he will find Frodo, but he will follow him.**

"You may meet a friend of mine on the Road: a Man, lean, dark, tall, by some called Strider. He knows our business and will help you."

c It is possible to say that Gandalf **doesn't know for sure if Frodo will meet Strider/describes his friend and says that everybody calls him Strider**.

d If Frodo finds Strider, it is possible to say that he **will surely help Frodo/may help Frodo**.

e "Will" is used when we talk about **plans and predictions/decisions made at the moment of speaking and predictions.**

2 **Now look at the picture and read some excerpts from the story of *The Lord of the Rings*: The Return of the King. Circle what you don't understand and discuss it with your classmates.**

Frodo Baggins and Sam Gamgee in the movie *The Lord of the Rings*: The Return of the King (2003)

I Frodo had no strength for such a battle. He sank to the ground. "I can't go on, Sam," he murmured. "I'm going to faint."

II "Bless me, Mr. Frodo, but you've gone and made me that hungry and thirsty," said Sam. "But if there's a drop of water left in my bottle, there's no more. That's not going to be enough for two..."

III "But what then, Sam Gamgee, what then? When you get there, what are you going to do?"

IV When all was at last ready Frodo said, "When are you going to move in and join me, Sam?"

V The first of Sam and Rosie's children was born on March 25. "Well, Sam", said Frodo, "Choose a flower like Rose. It must be a beautiful flower, because, you see, I think she is very beautiful, and is going to be beautifuller still."

Adapted from: TOLKIEN, John R. R. ***The Lord of the Rings:*** **The Return of the King**. London: HarperCollins Publishers, 2008. p. 104, 119, 148, 172, 173.

3 **Analyze the highlighted parts in the excerpts in activity 2. Then write their number according to what they describe.**

a ☐ Sam asks himself a question about his plans for a specific situation.
b ☐ Frodo makes a prediction about the future of Sam's baby.
c ☐ Frodo makes a prediction based on the fact that he is not well.
d ☐ Sam makes a prediction based on physical evidence.
e ☐ Frodo asks Sam about his plans of moving.

4 **Now, based on the highlighted parts from activity 2, match the sentences.**

a The negative sentences are formed by...

b The affirmative sentences are formed by...

c The interrogative sentences are formed by...

☐ subject + "am"/"is"/"are" + "going to" + main verb in the infinitive.
☐ (*wh-* word) + "am"/"is"/"are" + subject + "going to" + main verb in the infinitive.
☐ subject + "am"/"is"/"are" + "not" + "going to" + main verb in the infinitive.

5 **Based on the previous activities, circle the best option to complete these sentences.**

a When we make predictions for the future, we can use **"going to"/"will"/"going to" and "will"**.

b When we make predictions based on evidence, we use **"going to"/"will"/"going to" and "will"**.

c When we talk about plans for the future, we use **"going to"/"will"/"going to" and "will"**.

6 **Interview a partner. Discover his/her plans for the future and his/her predictions about his/her life.**

a What are your...

I plans for today after school? ______________________

II plans for next week? ______________________

III plans for your career? ______________________

IV plans for your personal life? ______________________

b What are your predictions for your life?

____

____

____

Useful language

I will/am going to... as soon as...
I'm going to... whatever happens.
I predict that...
I think...

Building blocks Means of communication

1 **Match the pictures to the means of communication.**

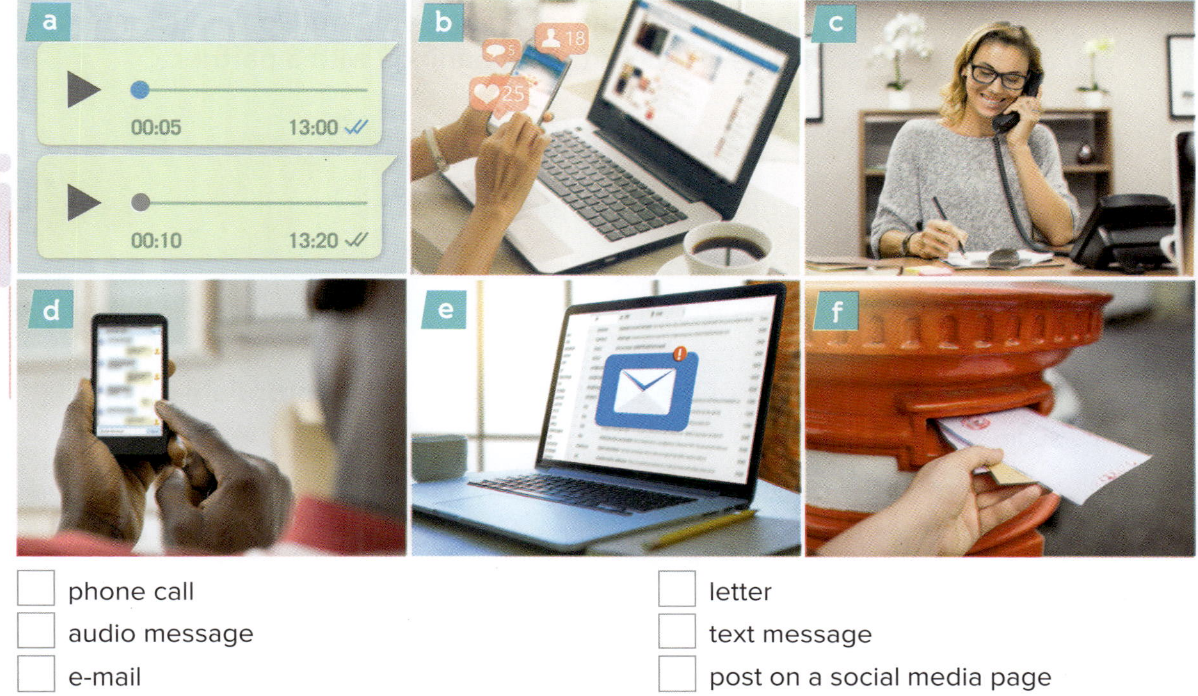

- [ ] phone call
- [ ] audio message
- [ ] e-mail
- [ ] letter
- [ ] text message
- [ ] post on a social media page

2 **Which means of communication would you prefer if you were in these situations? Use the vocabulary from activity 1.**

You need to...

contact someone quickly: ____________________

write long messages: ____________________

reach many people – even people you do not know: ____________________

3 **Look at the means of communication from activity 1 and check the possible problems each of them may have.**

	phone call	audio message	e-mail	letter	text message	post on a social media page
busy line						
slow internet speed						
undelivered mail						
poor signal						
low battery						

Watch:
Nonviolent communication

Sync Listening: Gestures in different cultures

Pre-listening

1 **In your opinion, what does each of these gestures mean? Do you use them when you are talking to someone? Discuss their meanings with a partner.**

a 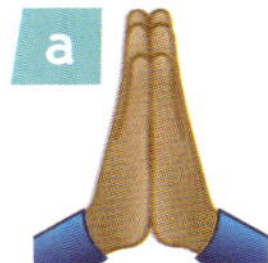
b 
c 
d 
e 
f 

Listening

2 14 **Listen to the first part of the audio and check the appropriate option.**

The audio is about...

a ☐ the history of some gestures around the world.
b ☐ different meanings for the same gestures around the world.
c ☐ universal gestures around the globe.

3 15 **Now look at the gestures represented in the pictures and listen to the second part of the audio about them. Then match the gestures to their meanings accordingly. They may have more than one meaning.**

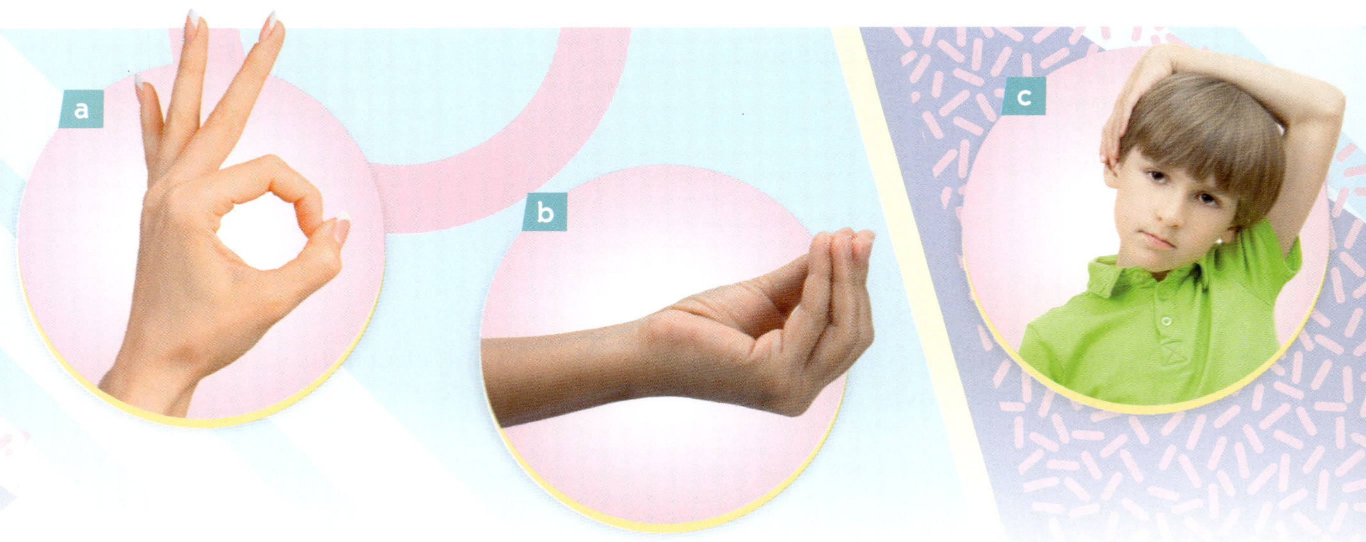

☐ It means "money".
☐ "Wait a second."
☐ "Everything is OK."
☐ "You are making things too complicated."
☐ It is used to emphasize something in speech.

4 15 **Now listen to the second part of the audio again and match the gestures in activity 3 to the places where they are used.**

1 ☐ Britain

2 ☐ Jordan

3 ☐ Japan

4 ☐ Italy

5 ☐ Russia

5 16 **Now listen to the third part of the audio and check the appropriate options.**

a What gestures do most people use to indicate "yes" and "no"?

☐ They nod for "yes" and shake their head for "no".
☐ They shake their head for "yes" and nod for "no".
☐ They use their tongue to make a click for "yes" and shake their head for "no".

b What gestures do Bulgarians use to indicate "yes" and "no"?

☐ They nod for "yes" and shake their head for "no".
☐ They shake their head for "yes" and nod with a click of the tongue for "no".
☐ They shake their head for "yes" and nod for "no".

Post-listening

6 **Read and decide if you agree (*A*) or disagree (*D*) with these statements. Then share your answers with your classmates.**

☐ Every culture sees the world in the same way.
☐ Each gesture can vary according to the context or culture.
☐ Some gestures that are OK in a country may be offensive in another.
☐ We should be aware of and respect cultural differences.

Sync Speaking: The future of communication

Pre-speaking

1 **Discuss these questions with a partner. Take notes if necessary.**

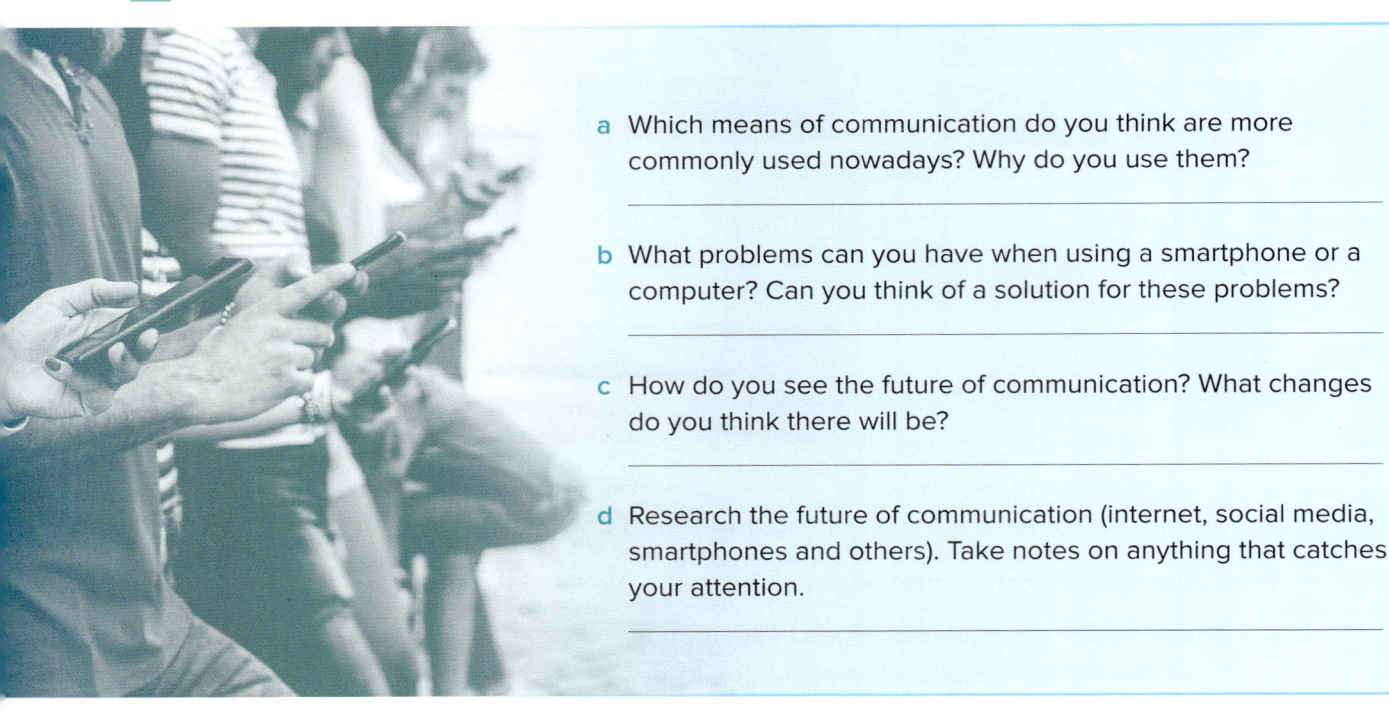

a Which means of communication do you think are more commonly used nowadays? Why do you use them?

____

b What problems can you have when using a smartphone or a computer? Can you think of a solution for these problems?

____

c How do you see the future of communication? What changes do you think there will be?

____

d Research the future of communication (internet, social media, smartphones and others). Take notes on anything that catches your attention.

____

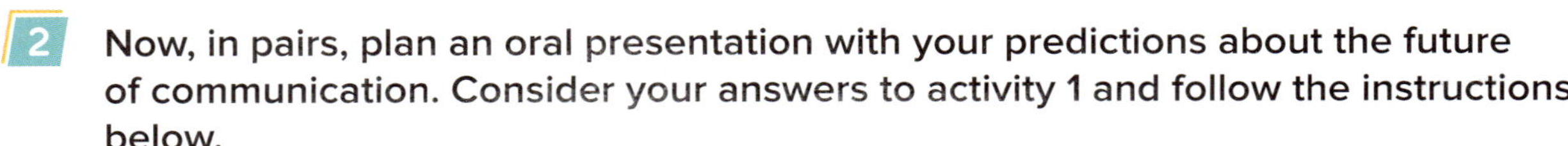

2 **Now, in pairs, plan an oral presentation with your predictions about the future of communication. Consider your answers to activity 1 and follow the instructions below.**

a Say how you think people will communicate in the future. What will be the positive and negative effects of technological advancements? Justify your answers.

b Rehearse your oral presentation with your partner. Be sure you are clear and calm during your speech.

Speaking

3 **Deliver your oral presentation.**

Post-speaking

4 **Discuss these questions with your classmates.**

a In your opinion, are the predictions made by your class plausible? Why? Which ones do you think are the closest to becoming reality?

b Which predictions do you like best? Why?

Studio Writing a letter about your dreams and plans

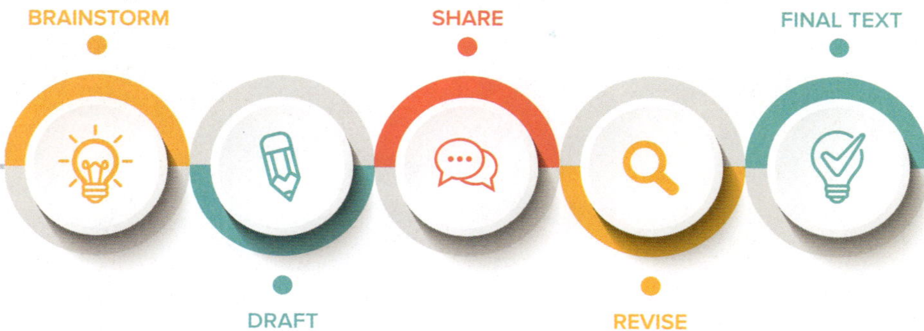

What: a letter about your dreams and plans for the future
To whom: the elderly
Media: paper
Objective: describe your dreams and plans for the future

1. **You are going to write a letter to an elderly person sharing your dreams and plans for the future. You are also going to ask them about their lives. Make a list of expressions about the future. What verb forms can you use to talk about plans and predictions?**
2. **Make sentences about your dreams and plans.**
3. **In pairs, think of what to ask someone about their lives and take notes.**
4. **Individually, write a letter to the elderly person about your dreams and plans for the future and how you intend to achieve them. Use the structure of the letter on page 89 as an example. Then create questions for the elderly, showing interest in his/her life. Ask for advice for your plans. Remember to use a clear and organized handwriting.**
5. **Read your letter and check if it shows interest in the recipient's life. Check if there is anything that might sound offensive in your text. Make any necessary corrections.**
6. **Exchange letters with a partner. Give and ask for feedback, making suggestions when needed.**
7. **Make adjustments to your letter according to the feedback received.**
8. **Once you have decided about the receiver, make sure to write his/her address correctly.**
9. **Talk to your classmates about your experience in writing a letter to an elderly person. How do you think the person will feel when he/she receives the letter?**

____

____

____

____

8 What's (in the) news?

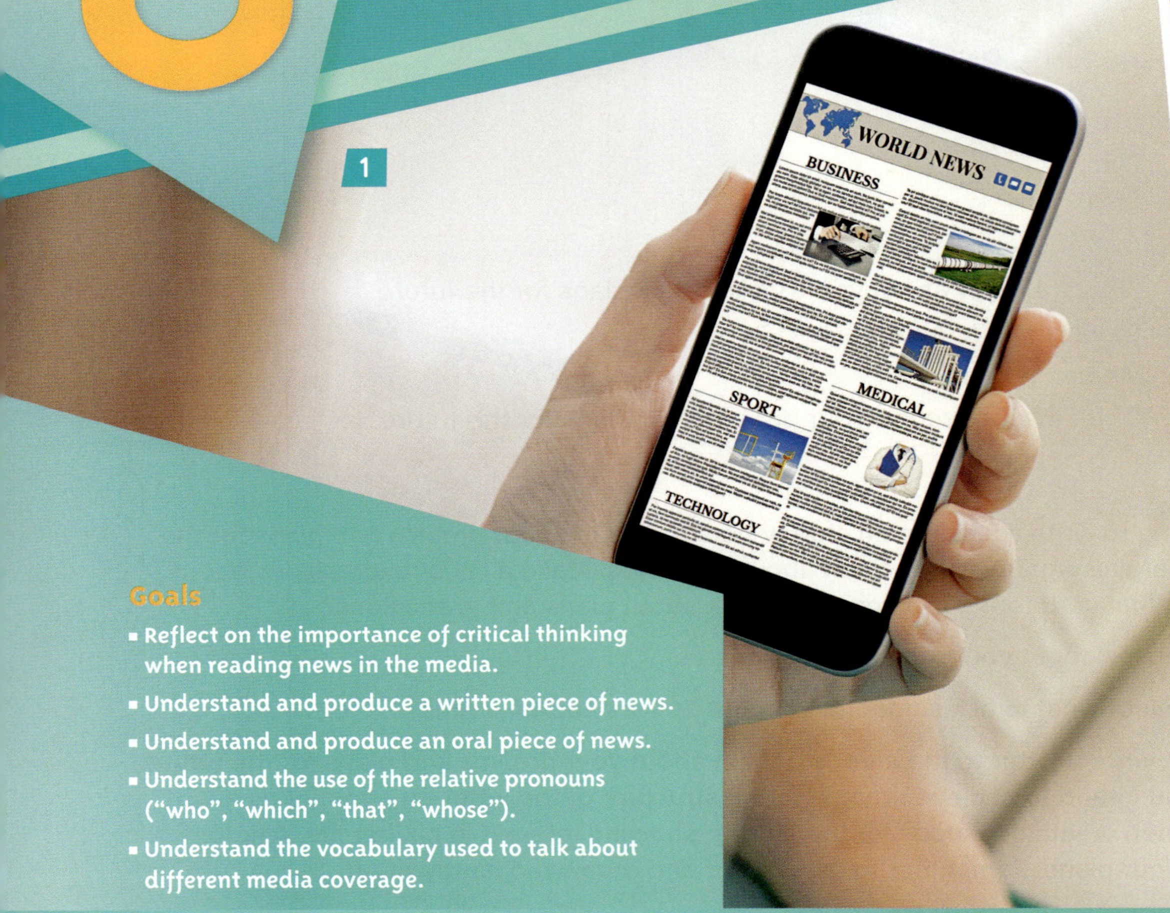

Goals

- Reflect on the importance of critical thinking when reading news in the media.
- Understand and produce a written piece of news.
- Understand and produce an oral piece of news.
- Understand the use of the relative pronouns ("who", "which", "that", "whose").
- Understand the vocabulary used to talk about different media coverage.

1 What does each picture show? Number the sentences according to the pictures.

- [ ] A family reading a newspaper.
- [ ] People watching the news on TV.
- [ ] Someone reading the news on a smartphone.
- [ ] Someone reading the news on a tablet.

2 What do the pictures have in common?

____

____

3 **Why is it important to keep up with the news? Check the most important reason/s for you.**

- [ ] To learn more about current events.
- [ ] To know what is going on around the world.
- [ ] To be well-informed and able to talk to people about different subjects.
- [ ] For entertainment.
- [ ] For habit.
- [ ] Other: ____________________

Explore News story

Pre-reading

1 **Read this poster. What is it about? Who produced it? What do you know about this subject?**

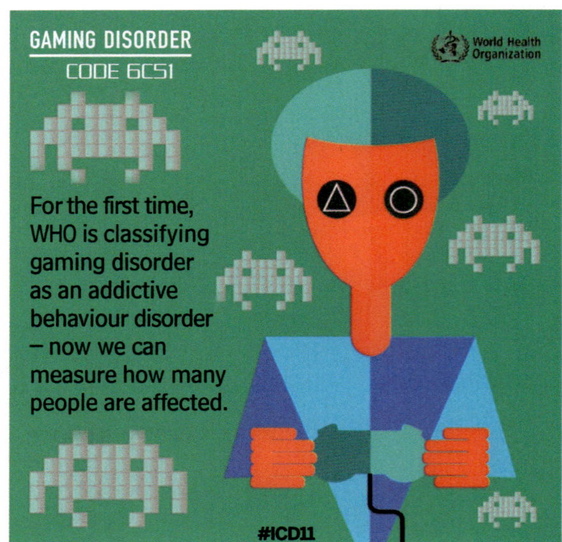

Available at <http://www.who.int/images/default-source/campaigns/international-classification-of-deseases/social-media-sqaures/icd-gaming-disorder.jpg>. Accessed on June 6, 2019.

> **Language clue**
>
> **Headline:** short title at the top of a newspaper article telling what it is about.
> **Source:** person, organization, book or document that provides information or evidence.

2 **Read these headlines and some first lines of news stories from newspapers from different countries. Which headlines are followed by the "lead" (opening paragraph of a news story)?**

Headline 1: South Africa

> **Gaming is now an addiction recognised by the World Health Organisation**
>
> PARENTS: The dangers, symptoms and solutions for online gaming addiction in all ages
>
> Laurie Smith

Zululand Observer, Empangeni, June 11, 2018.

Headline 2: South Korea

> **[Feature] Is game addiction a mental disorder? Korea's industry experts rebut WHO's labeling**
>
> By Sohn Ji-young

The Korea Herald, Seoul, March 28, 2018.

Headline 3: United Kingdom

> **"Dangerous gaming": is the WHO right to class excessive video game play as a health disorder?**
>
> Industry figures question research that 'pathologises' compulsive gaming, while scientist involved defends move to address addiction
>
> Jordan Erica Webber

The Guardian, London, February 5, 2018.

3 Read the headlines in activity 2 again and answer the questions.

a Which headline presents these perspectives? Number the statements accordingly.

- [ ] Shows opinions on both sides of the debate.
- [ ] Presents video games as something negative.
- [ ] Rebuts it (doesn't consider the classification to be true).

b What sources did the reporters probably consult to get information for their news stories?

____

Reading

4 Now read this news story. Which headline in activity 2 matches the text?

____

1 The World Health Organization (WHO) has included "gaming disorder" in its diagnostic manual, the International Classification of Diseases (ICD-11). The disorder is characterised by behaviours such as no control of time spent playing video games and prioritisation of gaming above other activities, negatively affecting other areas of a person's life such as their education, occupation and relationships.

2 Games industry bodies as the US Entertainment Software Association (ESA) and UK Interactive Entertainment (Ukie) have expressed doubts about the classification. "We are very concerned about the evidence that WHO is using to base this potential classification on," says Ukie's chief executive, Jo Twist.

3 Some researchers agree. "I just feel like we don't know enough yet," says Dr. Netta Weinstein, a senior lecturer in psychology at Cardiff University. "And we feel we know a lot."

4 According to a paper by researchers who were involved in the process, the WHO was initially exploring excessive use of the internet, computers and smartphones, but determined that the biggest concern was gaming. Reviews of the literature identified characteristics such as lack of control, increased priority, and continuation despite negative consequences. The authors write: "These features clearly have their parallels with addictions."

5 Weinstein is unconvinced. "In our research," she says, "we actually didn't find that symptoms correlated with health directly." And without the kinds of health effects you'd see in something like drug addiction, "it might be that something that we think of as addiction is actually just enthusiasm".

6 Prof. Mark Griffiths of Nottingham Trent University, who was part of the working party set up by the WHO to look into the classification, takes a firmer stance: "The bottom line is problematic gaming. Whether you call it 'gaming disorder' or 'gaming addiction', there is a minority of people out there where gaming has completely taken over their lives."

7 Weinstein has a concern about comorbidity (when a person has more than one condition): "We need to know that it is about the gaming itself, or we're treating something that's not the actual problem."

8 Twist agrees: "You have to look at pre-existing mental health disorders," she says.

9 The significance of the WHO's decision will depend on your point of view. Parents and governments could take it as justification for their discomfort with the younger generation's technological habits. But to a person who feels that their gaming behaviour is having a negative impact on their life, this official classification could offer a welcome step forward.

5 **Underline the appropriate options to complete the paragraph about the text in activity 4.**

The aim of the text is to present and **support WHO's decision/show opinions both for and against WHO's decision**. The journalist achieves this aim **by expressing other people's opinions about the topic/by not expressing opinions, just facts**.

6 **To present different perspectives, a journalist must consult different sources. Read the text in activity 4 again and complete the chart with a partner.**

Source	Occupation	Agrees/Disagrees with WHO
Jo Twist		
Dr. Netta Weinstein		
Prof. Mark Griffiths		

7 **Match the paragraphs 1-9 in the article to their functions.**

a ☐ To introduce the fact that became news.
b ☐ To present some of the consequences of this classification.
c ☐ To introduce the first argument against the classification.
d ☐ To mention a concern about comorbidity.
e ☐ To show that one of the researchers agrees on the concern about comorbidity.
f ☐ To introduce the first counterargument by a WHO team member.
g ☐ To introduce an opposing view, based on a psychologist's research.
h ☐ To point out that researchers still don't know enough about the topic.
i ☐ To quote a research paper as a source of information.

Post-reading

8 **Discuss these questions with your classmates.**

a How do you evaluate the information from the text? Why?

☐ Trustworthy.
☐ Moderately credible.
☐ Unreliable.

RTV

Watch:
Fake news

____

____

b Would you like to read more pieces of news about this topic?

☐ Yes, definitely.
☐ Maybe.
☐ Definitely not.

Building blocks Words used in the news industry

1 **Which sources can we use to get information? Label the pictures using the phrases in the box.**

a digital billboard   a newspaper   a radio program   a social media network   a TV news program   a variable message sign

a

b

c

d

e

f
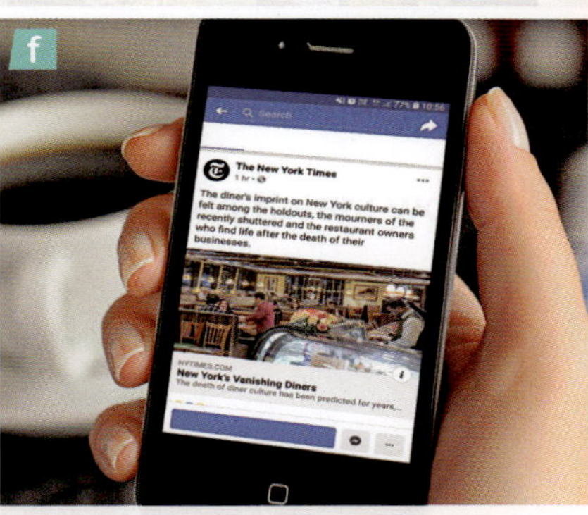

2 **Answer the questions with a partner.**

a Which type of media from activity 1 can be used to broadcast or display...

I road alerts? __________

II breaking news? __________

III weather forecasts? __________

b Which items in activity 1 do you usually use to get informed?

____

Language clue

"News" is an uncountable noun. Observe: This **is** the **news**. I have **two pieces of news** to tell you.

Toolbox Relative pronouns

1 **Read these headlines of newspapers from around the world. Which story/stories would you like to read?**

Headline 1: Australia

Strange platypus-like fish discovered in Australia's ancient reef system

Headline 2: Indonesia

Environmental group aims to plant two million trees on Mount Rinjani

Headline 3: United Arab Emirates

Refugee children to go back to school with a little help from the UAE

Headline 4: United States

Beluga whales have sensitive hearing, little age-related loss

2 **Now match each extract to the corresponding headline in activity 1.**

a "Young people whose education has been interrupted by conflict deserve a chance to rebuild their lives and have a shot at a good future."

Available at <https://www.thenational.ae/uae/refugee-children-to-go-back-to-school-with-a-little-help-from-the-uae-1.742208>. Accessed on March 22, 2019.

____

b "The two studies are important to efforts to evaluate the effects of underwater noise on endangered beluga whales, whose numbers have reduced to an estimated 328."

Adapted from <https://www.sciencedaily.com/releases/2018/06/180620100617.htm>. Accessed on March 22, 2019.

____

c "The fossils, which belong to an extinct group called the placoderms, were first discovered in 1980. Gavin Young, who has spent more than 50 years researching fossil fish from the lake, said the find was certainly the weirdest and most specialised example."

Adapted from <https://www.news.com.au/technology/science/archaeology/strange-platypuslike-fish-discovered-in-australias-ancient-reef-system/news-story/8cbafa8ce5fb04d8d6c0830ec2a0a387>. Accessed on March 22, 2019.

____

d "The event will see tree seedlings distributed to thousands of people who reside in the five districts in North Lombok."

Adapted from ***The Jakarta Post***, Mataram, December 11, 2017.

____

3 Analyze the highlighted words in the extracts in activity 2. Then underline the appropriate options.

a The relative pronouns "who" and "which" come **after/before** a noun. They make reference to an element that **has already been mentioned/has not been mentioned yet** in the sentence.

b The relative pronoun "whose" comes before a **noun/verb** and expresses possession.

c The relative pronoun "**who**"/"**which**" is used when we talk about human subjects.

d The relative pronoun "**who**"/"**which**" is used when we talk about nonhuman subjects (things, animals etc.).

e The relative pronoun "whose" **can/cannot** be used to refer to both human and nonhuman subjects.

4 Read these sentences. What pronoun is replacing "which" and "who"? Circle.

It is a game that pleases the children and adults in the audience.
We have an idea of the people that like this kind of news.

5 Read these extracts from activity 2 again and check the appropriate options.

"The fossils, which belong to an extinct group called the placoderms, were first discovered in 1980. Gavin Young, who has spent more than 50 years researching fossil fish from the lake, said the find was certainly the weirdest and most specialised example."

a The highlighted clauses offer ________ understand the news item.

☐ essential information to ☐ extra information. If they are omitted, we can still

b The highlighted clauses ________ between commas.

☐ come ☐ don't come

"The event will see tree seedlings distributed to thousands of people who reside in the five districts in North Lombok."

c The highlighted clause offers ________ understand the news item.

☐ essential information to ☐ extra information. If it is omitted, we can still

d The highlighted clause ________ between commas.

☐ comes ☐ doesn't come

Language clue

In "extra information clauses" we **cannot** replace "who" or "which" with "that".

6 Complete the questions with a relative pronoun. Then discuss them with a partner.

a Are there any news programs ________________ you can't stand? Why don't you like them?

b Are news presenters ________________ usually make personal comments about the news more interesting?

c Can you name any radio programs ________________ listeners can participate live?

Sync Listening: A TV news story

Pre-listening

1 **Read the headlines from a TV news story and from a newspaper. How are they different?**

15-year-old schoolgirl invents biodegradable plastic!

Turning prawns into plastic: Schoolgirl Angelina Arora fights science stereotypes

The Sydney Morning Herald, Sydney, December 8, 2017.

Language clue

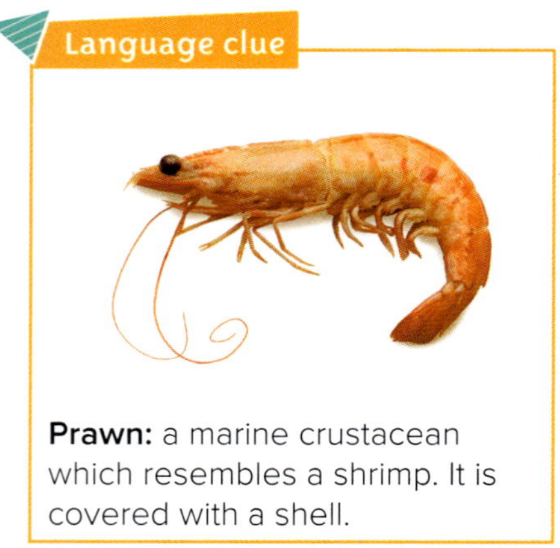

Prawn: a marine crustacean which resembles a shrimp. It is covered with a shell.

____

____

____

2 **Based on activity 1, think about the TV news story on Angelina Arora and do the activities with a partner.**

Choose the topics you think the news story will probably cover.

- [ ] Where Angelina is from.
- [ ] Where she studies.
- [ ] Who helped her with the invention.
- [ ] How she made her invention.
- [ ] What she is going to do next.
- [ ] When she invented the biodegradable plastic.

3 **Now use your ideas from activity 2 and circle the words and phrases you think might be mentioned in the audio.**

biodegradable plastic   chair   corn starch   fish   landfills
plastic waste   prawn shells   seals   silk cocoons   spiders' web

Listening

4 17 **Listen to the news story and check your predictions in activities 2 and 3.**

5 17 **Listen to the audio again and underline the appropriate options.**

a Angelina created her plastic to help clean **the oceans/the forests**.

b Her plastic starts to break down within **five/fifteen** days and completely breaks down in 33 **days/months**.

c **Her teacher/The school principal** supervised her work.

d She first started experimenting in **2013/2016**.

e She used corn starch to create a biodegradable plastic, but it was **resistant/not resistant** to water.

f She **won/didn't win** a prize for her first project.

g Angelina's teacher says she is **hard-working/intelligent**.

h **Austria/Australia** produces a lot of seafood waste.

i Her invention **helps/doesn't help** reduce waste in landfills.

j Angelina says **age/gender** shouldn't be a limit to invention and discovery.

Post-listening

6 **Complete this summary of how Angelina created her bioplastic using prawn shells. Use words/expressions from activity 3.**

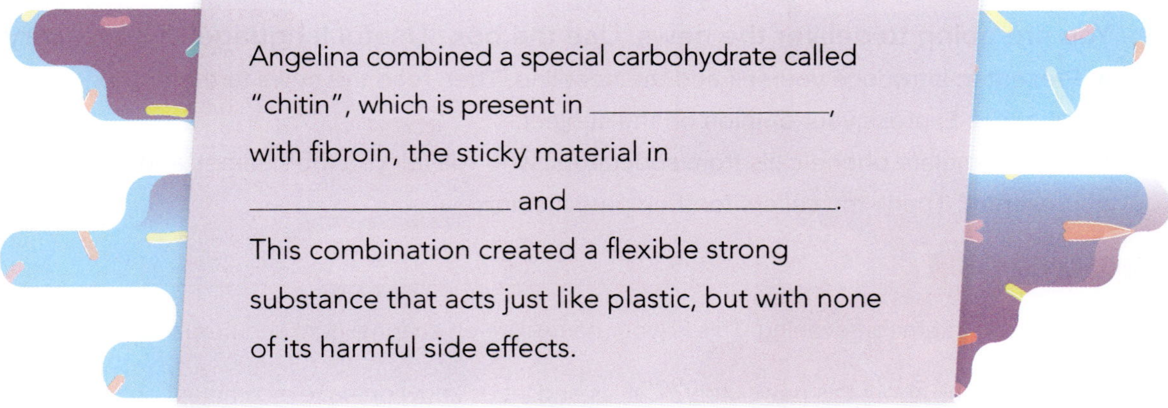

Angelina combined a special carbohydrate called "chitin", which is present in ________________, with fibroin, the sticky material in ________________ and ________________. This combination created a flexible strong substance that acts just like plastic, but with none of its harmful side effects.

7 **Discuss these questions with a partner and answer them.**

a Which local or global problem would you like to solve?

____

____

b How would you do it?

____

____

Sync Speaking: This is the news

Pre-speaking

1 **In your opinion, what qualities must a good news presenter have?**

____

2 **Let's prepare a TV news report.**

a Get into small groups. Decide on a news item that is relevant for your community. Think about the different perspectives you could focus on.

b Find facts and opinions about it in different media and select the most relevant pieces of information and sources.

c Write the news story, including quotations to support what you are saying, and a final comment to express the group's opinion.

d Decide on the roles: the news presenter and the source/s.

e Practice reading your stories aloud and listen to the other groups as well. Give and receive feedback. Review your text if necessary.

Speaking

3 **You are going to deliver the news. Use the box "Useful language" if necessary.**

a Presenter: Introduce yourself and the headline. Then read the news to the group.

b Source/s: Express your opinion on the subject.

c Class: Simulate phone calls from spectators, who will tell you their names and what they think.

d Presenter: Thank the callers for their participation.

Useful language

Good morning/afternoon/evening. This is (your name) live on channel (ten) and here's our top story/today's news.
What do you think about this news story? Call us and let us know or leave a comment on our webpage.

Post-speaking

4 **Discuss these questions with your classmates.**

a How do you rate your presentation?

- [ ] excellent
- [ ] very good
- [ ] pretty good
- [ ] OK
- [ ] a little disappointing

b How do you rate your classmates' news stories?

- [ ] excellent
- [ ] very good
- [ ] pretty good
- [ ] OK
- [ ] a little disappointing

c Would you like to record your news story on a video or podcast? Why?

What: a news story for a school newspaper
To whom: other students; people in general
Media: paper; digital
Objective: report and inform the community about an important issue

1. Work in groups. List facts and events that are happening in your community.
2. Choose a topic and decide what sources will be checked.
3. Collect material: interviews, notes, research, pictures.
4. Write the news story. Remember to include: a headline, a lead summarizing the news (who/what/when/why), a body with quotations and a conclusion.
5. Think of the format of the news story: fonts, sizes, pictures and distribution.
6. Share your text with your classmates. Give and receive feedback on content and form.
7. Revise your production according to the feedback received. Rewrite the text, adding, correcting or deleting information.
8. Finish the text and remember that it should look like a newspaper page.
9. Share your final version with your classmates.
10. Collect all the texts to create a class newspaper. Leave a copy at the school library or on a bulletin board. Invite other people to read and discuss the news. Publish your work on the **Students for PEACE Social Media** <www.studentsforpeace.com.br>, using the tag **newsstory** or others chosen by the students.

Peace talk

Chapters 7 and 8
E-safety issues

1 Read these statements about technology and tell a partner if you agree or disagree with them.

a Most teenagers use digital technology well and autonomously, so they don't need to learn new things from adults.

b It is important to develop new skills and knowledge to use digital technology, even if we can use it successfully.

c Digital technology has its dangers and we need to know how to deal with them.

2 Look at the pictures and answer the questions. Then discuss them with your classmates.

1

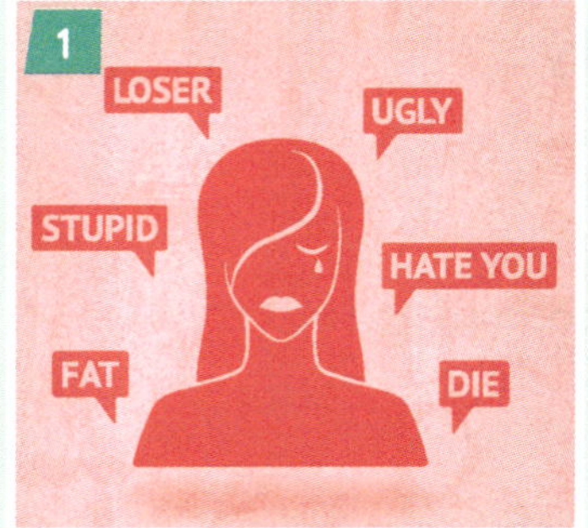

2

3

a What is the general problem you can identify in the three pictures? And what specific problem does each picture represent?

___

___

___

b Have you (or has anyone you know) ever been involved in a situation related to these types of problem? If so, could you share it with the class?

___

___

___

c How careful are you when you use the internet? How do you stay safe online? What tips can you share with your classmates?

___

___

___

3 Match the items related to online interactions to their definitions.

a Cyber abuse/Trolling/Cyber harassment/Cyberbullying...

b Image-based abuse...

c Personal information...

d Digital citizenship...

☐ is a term we use to refer to positive and conscious use of digital technology.

☐ refers to a situation in which intimate pictures (real or edited) are shared without the permission of the person in them.

☐ is an online behavior that often involves a seriously intimidating, threatening or humiliating effect on someone. It is intended to hurt this person socially, psychologically or physically.

☐ refers to any type of information or combination of information that makes the identification of an individual possible.

4 Read this excerpt from a book that covers several topics related to e-safety. Based on the introductory paragraph and the bulleted sentences, what type of text is this?

As with all school equipment, there are rules in place to keep both students and staff safe. It is important that students read and understand these rules.

- I will not install any programmes on school computers.
- I will not use the internet to cause distress or to bully others.
- I will not post pictures or videos to the internet, or otherwise upload content, unless under staff supervision.
- I will report any known misuses of technology, including the unacceptable behaviours of others.
- I will keep my computer and e-mail passwords private and will not use other students' passwords.
- I will not make, or attempt to make, any changes to school computer systems and settings.
- I will not use the internet to gain access to materials which are illegal, inappropriate or abusive.
- I am aware that the school has software installed on school computers to monitor student use.

Adapted from GIANT, Nikki. ***E-safety for the I-generation:* Combating the Misuse and Abuse of Technology in Schools.** Philadelphia: Jessica Kingsley Publishers, 2013. p. 126.

5 Now create an "e-safety tips list" with your classmates. Use the text in activity 4 as reference.

1 Form groups. Create a poster to show people how to stay safe online.

2 Think about the audience of your poster: your classmates, other people at school or people outside school?

3 Write your list, using the text in activity 4 as a reference. Remember to illustrate the content with pictures.

4 Display your poster.

Self-assessment

Chapter 1 – In the future

Can you read, understand and create a microblog post?
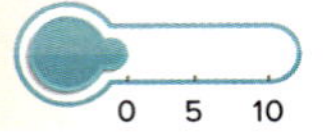
0 5 10

Can you understand and use the future tense with "will"?
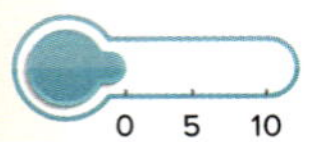
0 5 10

Can you understand and use adverbs to talk about the future?
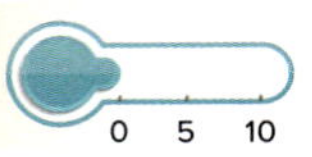
0 5 10

Can you understand an audio about the future?
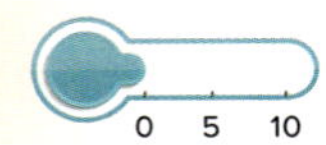
0 5 10

Chapter 2 – Health

Can you understand and use vocabulary about health?
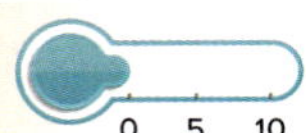
0 5 10

Can you read, understand and create a personal story?
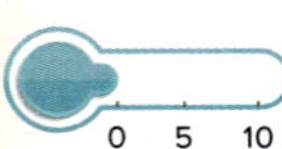
0 5 10

Can you understand and use "some", "any", "many" and "much"?
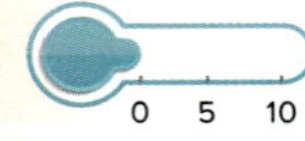
0 5 10

Can you understand and use affixes?
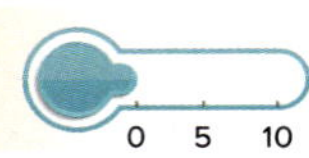
0 5 10

Chapter 3 – Time to celebrate!

Can you understand and use the present simple?
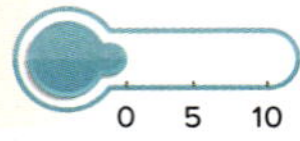
0 5 10

Can you read, understand and create an informational text about a celebration?
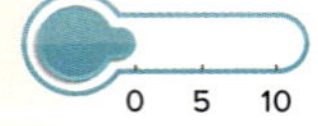
0 5 10

Can you understand and produce an oral text about traditional songs?
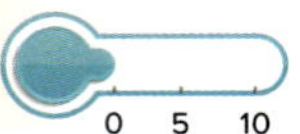
0 5 10

Can you understand and use dates in English?
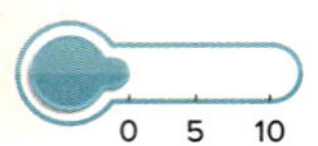
0 5 10

Chapter 4 – Art

Can you read and understand an informational text about an artwork?
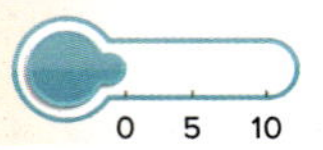
0 5 10

Can you understand and use the comparative form of the adjectives?
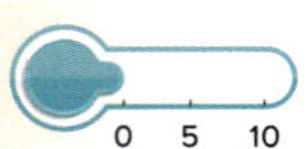
0 5 10

Can you understand and use vocabulary related to kinds of art?
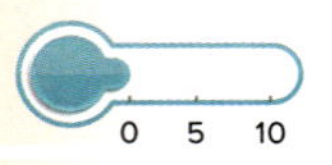
0 5 10

Can you understand and create an audio guide describing a work of art?
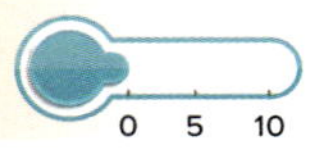
0 5 10

Chapter 5 – Movie world

Can you understand the main ideas of a movie synopsis and its reviews?
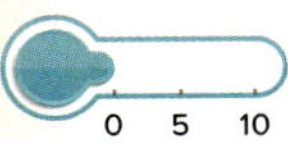
0 5 10

Can you understand and use the superlative form of the adjectives?
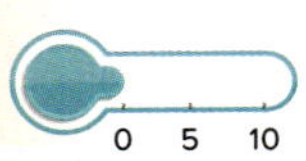
0 5 10

Can you understand and give an oral opinion about movies?
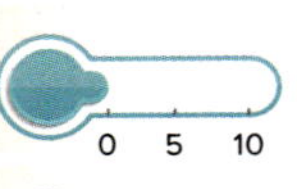
0 5 10

Can you write a short movie review?
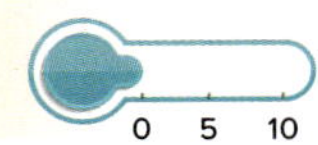
0 5 10

Chapter 6 – From cover to cover

Can you read and understand excerpts from literary pieces?
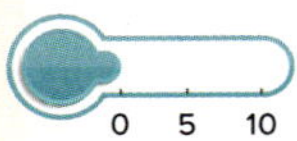
0 5 10

Can you identify the main literary genres?
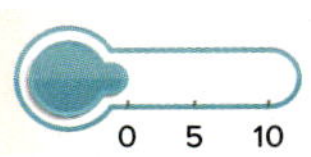
0 5 10

Can you understand and use verbs in the past simple and the past continuous tenses?
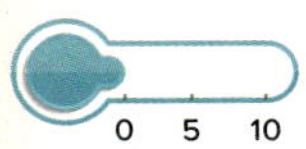
0 5 10

Can you give an oral presentation about a book?

0 5 10

Chapter 7 – Communication

Can you understand and use "will" and "going to" to refer to the future?
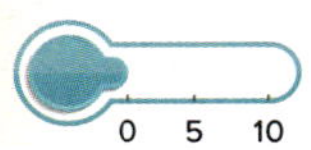
0 5 10

Can you make predictions about the future of communication?
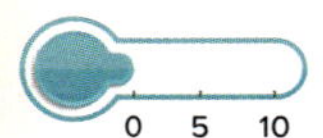
0 5 10

Can you understand the meanings of different gestures and expressions in different cultures?
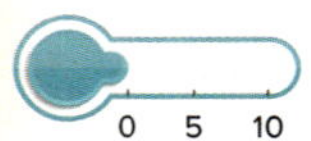
0 5 10

Can you write a letter telling someone about your future plans and dreams and asking about this person's plans and dreams?
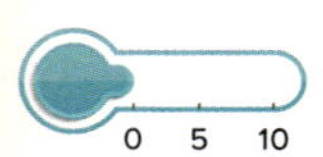
0 5 10

Chapter 8 – What's (in the) news?

Can you understand and produce a written piece of news?
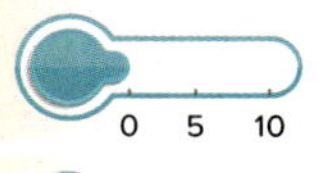
0 5 10

Can you understand the vocabulary to talk about different media coverage?
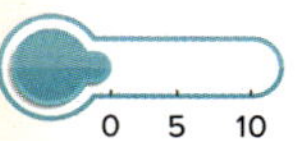
0 5 10

Can you understand the use of the relative pronouns "who", "which", "that" and "whose"?
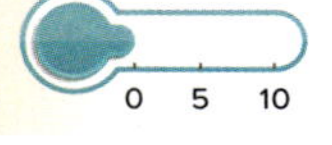
0 5 10

Can you understand and produce an oral piece of news?
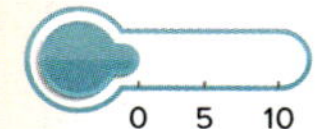
0 5 10

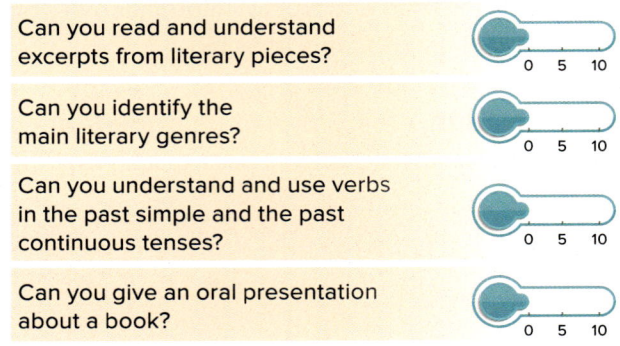

Workbook

Name: ______________________ Class: __________ Date: __________

Chapter 1 In the future

1 **Look at some tweets derived from Greta Thunberg's speech at the UK Parliament. Complete the texts with the appropriate future form of the verbs in parentheses.**

a

CarolSmith
@CarolSmith 19h

My second week! "Mass media are silent about global warming, but we ______________ (suffer)." Difficult to translate it better. #climatestrike #FridaysForFuture

11:30 AM 10 May 2019

5 Retweets 21 Likes

5 21

b

KatieP
@KatieP 11h

I agree with Greta! We ______________ (not/understand) it until it's too late… Those who ______________ (be) affected the hardest are already suffering the consequences. #climatestrike #FridaysForFuture

8:00 AM 12 May 2019

9 Retweets 15 Likes

9 15

c

MichaelS
@MichaelS 6h

This cloudy morning, we ______________ (stand) on the road in Budapest to #ClimateStrike to seek attention to my message "WE ______________ (save) OUR FUTURE #KeepMamaAfricaGreen". Our Earth ______________ (not/disappear). #FridaysForFuture @GretaThunberg @Fridays4FutureU

8:00 AM 12 May 2019

9 Retweets 15 Likes

9 15

d

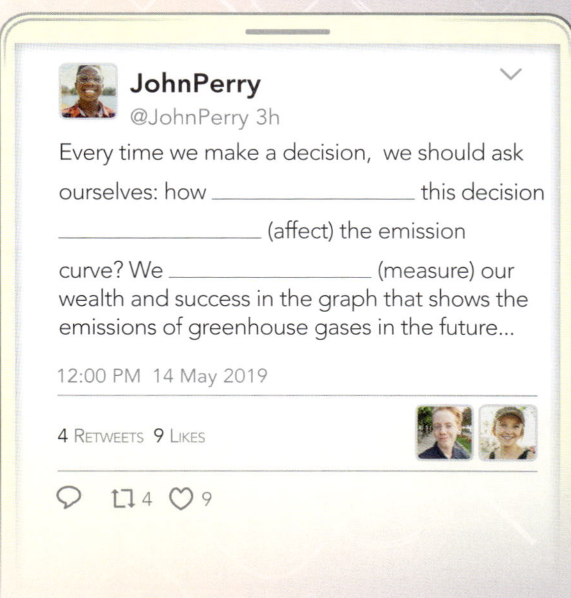

JohnPerry
@JohnPerry 3h

Every time we make a decision, we should ask ourselves: how ______________ this decision ______________ (affect) the emission curve? We ______________ (measure) our wealth and success in the graph that shows the emissions of greenhouse gases in the future...

12:00 PM 14 May 2019

4 Retweets 9 Likes

4 9

2 Read the tweets in activity 1 again. Which ones...

a have hashtags? ______

b talk about negative consequences of climate change? ______

c talk about the protest itself? ______

d would you reply to? ______

3 Read this article about humanity in the future. Complete the blanks with the future form of the verbs in parentheses. Decide if the sentences are affirmative or negative, according to the context. You may use contractions.

It's easy to believe that the human race ______ (be) around for long when you consider the state of the world nowadays. But we always try to be positive. That's why we've asked several people this month to envision what humans ______ (look like) in 100 years.

Mark Johnson imagines technology as a positive force rather than one that ______ (destroy) us. Maybe we ______ (try) our best to have a global cleanup. Or maybe we ______ (use) augmented reality to build empathy and conserve resources.

Maria Chimisky says, "In the future, gender, physical makeup, body structure, facial structure and skin tone ______ (be) customizable, because we ______ always ______ (wear) augmented reality simulators. This ______ (revolutionize) our impact on the planet, making everything more sustainable and limitless.".

Jay Nolan says nature ______ (change) us much, but with the help of our scientific community, we ______ (help) our bodies last longer and endure more. Who knows? Which way ______ we ______ (go)?

Based on <https://medium.com/s/futurehuman/will-humanity-be-better-off-in-2118-d1b2b44cd998>. Accessed on March 18, 2019.

4 Read these questions about the future and complete them with the future form of the verbs in parentheses. Then give your own answers.

a ______ we ______ (find) extraterrestrial life?

______

b ______ the world ______ (have) adequate health care one day?

______

c ______ technology ______ (eliminate) the need for animal testing?

______

d ______ gender equality ______ (be) achieved in the sciences?

______

Adapted from <https://www.scientificamerican.com/article/20-big-questions-about-the-future-of-humanity/>. Accessed on April 22, 2019.

Workbook Name: ________________ Class: ________ Date: ________

Chapter 2 Health

1 **Look at the pictures. Complete the sentences with *some*, *any*, *much* or *many*.**

a

There are ________________ types of bread in this picture. There are certainly ________________ healthy options among them.

b

Of course you can make a sandwich! There is ________________ bread left. But don't eat everything: consuming too ________________ carbs is not recommendable!

c

You'd better hurry up and go to the market. There isn't ________________ food left for your dog.

d

I don't think you have ________________ time before the exam finishes.

e

People won't see ________________ dogs here. They are not allowed in this park.

f

They don't have ________________ money yet, but they will save ________________ every month.

2 Complete these tips for taking care of your body. Use *some*, *any*, *many* or *much*.

There are __________ ways to take care of yourself physically and mentally. You don't need __________ money to improve your health. Here are __________ things you can do:

- Eat __________ nutritious food every day.
- Avoid cigarettes – you don't need __________ to be happy!
- Drink plenty of water.
- Do __________ exercise, which helps decrease depression and anxiety and improves moods.
- Sleep well. Not getting __________ sleep is harmful. Studies show that not sleeping enough contributes to a high rate of depression in __________ people.

Adapted from <https://www.uhs.umich.edu/tenthings>. Accessed on April 23, 2019.

3 Read this text about sugar and circle the appropriate options to complete it.

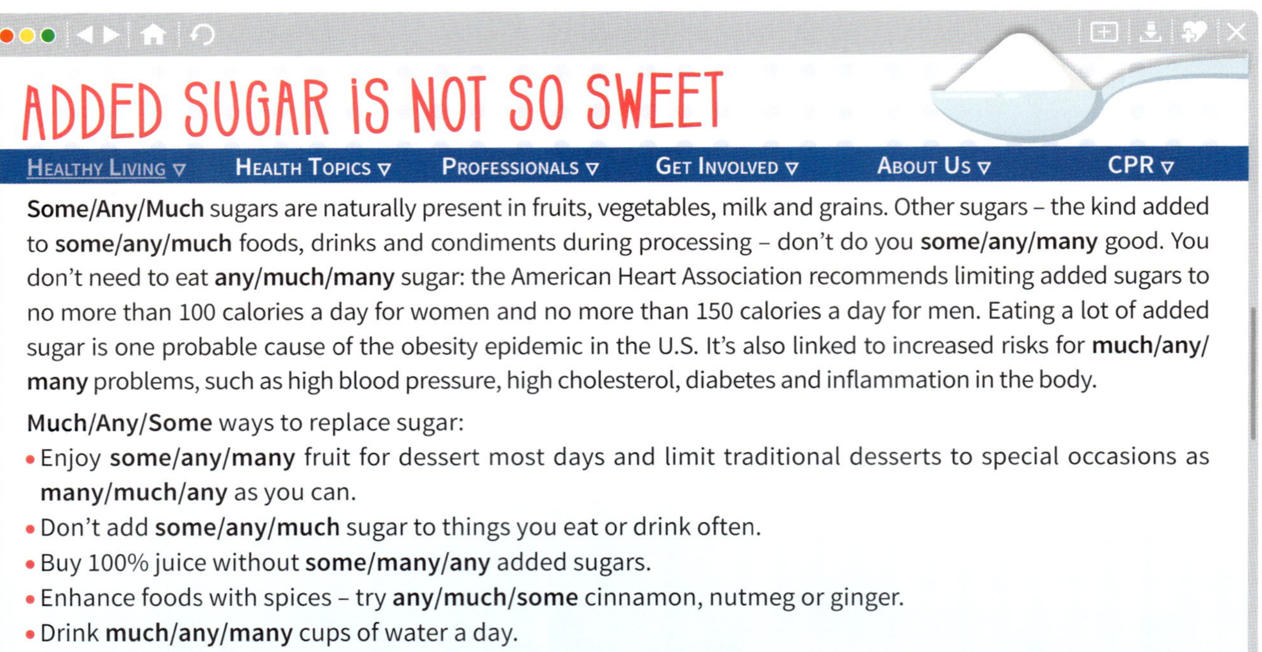

ADDED SUGAR IS NOT SO SWEET

HEALTHY LIVING ▽ HEALTH TOPICS ▽ PROFESSIONALS ▽ GET INVOLVED ▽ ABOUT US ▽ CPR ▽

Some/Any/Much sugars are naturally present in fruits, vegetables, milk and grains. Other sugars – the kind added to **some/any/much** foods, drinks and condiments during processing – don't do you **some/any/many** good. You don't need to eat **any/much/many** sugar: the American Heart Association recommends limiting added sugars to no more than 100 calories a day for women and no more than 150 calories a day for men. Eating a lot of added sugar is one probable cause of the obesity epidemic in the U.S. It's also linked to increased risks for **much/any/many** problems, such as high blood pressure, high cholesterol, diabetes and inflammation in the body.

Much/Any/Some ways to replace sugar:

- Enjoy **some/any/many** fruit for dessert most days and limit traditional desserts to special occasions as **many/much/any** as you can.
- Don't add **some/any/much** sugar to things you eat or drink often.
- Buy 100% juice without **some/many/any** added sugars.
- Enhance foods with spices – try **any/much/some** cinnamon, nutmeg or ginger.
- Drink **much/any/many** cups of water a day.
- Don't drink **some/any/many** sweetened tea nor sugar beverages.

Adapted from <https://www.heart.org/en/healthy-living/healthy-eating/eat-smart/sugar/added-sugars>; <https://www.heart.org/en/healthy-living/healthy-eating/eat-smart/sugar/cut-out-added-sugars-infographic>. Accessed on April 23, 2019.

4 Now write some sentences about health using *some*, *any*, *much* or *many*.

a __________

b __________

c __________

d __________

e __________

Name: __________________ Class: __________ Date: __________

Chapter 3 Time to celebrate!

1 **Read the texts about one of Mexico's most famous holidays, the Day of the Dead, and the Taiwan Lantern Festival. Complete them with the appropriate form of the verbs in parentheses.**

a The celebration of the lives of ancestors __________________ (be) present in Mexican culture. The country __________________ (celebrate) the Day of the Dead on November 2nd. People __________________ (say) it is when the dead __________________ (have) permission to visit their living relatives and friends. Mexicans __________________ (decorate) their homes with flowers, candles and incense. The whole country __________________ (celebrate) this visit with food, music and sweets. In the streets, there are parades of people who __________________ (dress up) in costumes and __________________ (wear) masks with painted skeletons.

b The Taiwan Lantern Festival __________________ (take place) on the first full moon of the Lunar New Year, and __________________ (have) everything from electric-powered lantern shows to more traditional events, like the Pingxi Sky Lantern Festival. In Pingxi, outside of the capital Taipei, villagers __________________ (let go) paper lanterns into the sky. Locals and visitors __________________ (like) the practice because they believe it __________________ (give) them good luck in the New Year.

Based on <https://www.momondo.com/inspiration/events-around-the-world/>. Accessed on March 19, 2019.

2 **Look at the chart. Which festivals are not celebrated in a specific date?**

January	Chinese New Year	between 01/21 and 02/20
February	Holi	between the end of February and the middle of March
March	Tolkien Reading Day	03/25
April	Shakespeare Day	04/23
June	World Environment Day	06/05

____

3 **Go back to the chart in activity 2. Ask and answer questions about celebrations around the world.**

a (Chinese/New Year)

When do the Chinese celebrate the New Year? They celebrate it between January 21st and February 20th.

b (Indian/Holi)

____

c (British/Tolkien Reading Day)

____

d (British/Shakespeare Day)

____

e (people/World Environment Day)

____

4 **Read about an important Muslim celebration. Then write *T* (true) or *F* (false) and correct the false statements.**

EID AL-FITR
THE END OF A
30-DAY FAST

Eid al-Fitr means "Festival of Breaking the Fast". It is a three-day celebration observed by Muslims worldwide. On this religious holiday, Muslims celebrate the end of Ramadan, a 30-day dawn-to-sunset fast. On the first day of Eid al-Fitr, the community gets together for prayer and a sermon. After this gathering, families and friends eat breakfast together, the first meal they eat in daylight after a whole month. Children receive gifts, people donate to charities, visit their families and go to cemeteries to honor their ancestors.

Adapted from <https://www.familysearch.org/blog/en/holidays-around-the-world/>. Accessed on April 22, 2019.

a ☐ Muslims all over the world celebrate Eid al-Fitr.

____

b ☐ For 30 days, Muslims only eat during the day.

____

c ☐ People don't give gifts to children on Eid al-Fitr.

____

d ☐ The celebration of Eid al-Fitr lasts for three days.

____

e ☐ The Ramadan is a three-day celebration.

____

f ☐ On Eid al-Fitr, Muslims visit their families and cemeteries and donate to charities.

____

Workbook

Name: ______________________ Class: __________ Date: __________

Chapter 4 Art

1 **Read the descriptions of famous sculptures and match them to their corresponding pictures.**

a

b

c

d

☐ It is a bronze statue by Edvard Eriksen (1876-1959), depicting a mermaid becoming human. The sculpture is displayed on a rock by the waterside at the Langelinie promenade in Copenhagen, Denmark. It is 1.25 m tall and weighs 175 kilograms. It turned 100 years old in 2013.

Based on <https://www.visitcopenhagen.com/copenhagen/little-mermaid-gdk586951>; <https://www.visitdenmark.com/denmark/little-mermaid-denmarks-most-photographed-statue>; <https://en.wikipedia.org/wiki/The_Little_Mermaid_(statue)>. Accessed on April 26, 2019.

☐ Marble statue of an athlete stooping to throw the discus. One of several Roman copies made of a lost bronze original made in the 5th century BC by the sculptor Myron. The head is wrongly restored and should be turned to watch the discus. Height: 1.7 meters.

Available at <https://www.britishmuseum.org/research/collection_online/collection_object_details.aspx?objectId=8760&partId=1&searchText=The+Townley+Discobolus&page=1>. Accessed on April 26, 2019.

☐ It is a colossal seated figure sculpted by Daniel Chester French (1850-1931) and carved by the Piccirilli Brothers. It is situated in the Lincoln Memorial (constructed between the years 1914 and 1922) on the National Mall, Washington, D.C., United States, and was unveiled in 1922. Stylistically, the work follows the Beaux Arts and American Renaissance traditions. Chamber floor to top of statue: 9.1 meters. Statue: 28 pieces. Height: 5.7912 meters. Weight: 120 tons (175 tons with the pedestal).

Adapted from <https://www.nps.gov/linc/learn/historyculture/lincoln-memorial-building-statistics.htm>. Accessed on April 26, 2019.

☐ It is a marble sculpture that was likely created by Alexandros of Antioch during the late 2nd century BC. It features a nearly nude, larger-than-life (about 2 meters tall) female figure posed in a classical S-curve. The figure is widely believed to be the goddess of love.

Based on <https://mymodernmet.com/venus-de-milo-statue/>; <https://en.wikipedia.org/wiki/Venus_de_Milo>. Accessed on April 26, 2019.

2 Complete the chart with information from the sculptures in activity 1. Then write sentences using comparatives.

Name	When it was created	Height	Weight	Location
Venus de Milo			–	Paris, France
The Little Mermaid				
Abraham Lincoln				
The Townley Discobolus			–	London, United Kingdom

a Tall: Venus de Milo x Abraham Lincoln

____

b Old: The Townley Discobolus x The Little Mermaid

____

c New: Abraham Lincoln x The Little Mermaid

____

d Far from us: Venus de Milo x Abraham Lincoln

____

e Light: Abraham Lincoln x The Little Mermaid

____

f Interesting: The Townley Discobolus x Abraham Lincoln

____

g Beautiful: The Little Mermaid x Venus de Milo

____

3 Read these sentences about women in art. Complete them with the appropriate comparative form of the adjectives in parentheses.

a The stereotyped idea that women aren't good artists really makes it ______________ (hard) for their work to be appreciated.

b When a work of art is signed by a woman, its price is ______________ (cheap). Because of that, female artists are ______________ (likely) to leave their work unsigned.

c The Tate Britain museum has a 30% cap on the collection of female artists, and its annual budget is even ______________ (bad), with as little as 13% spent on works by female artists in recent years.

d Female creatives were ______________ (successful) in the 1990s than they are now.

Based on <www.theguardian.com/commentisfree/2018/aug/13/tate-female-artists-museum-diversity-acquisitions-art-collect>. Accessed on May 5, 2019.

Workbook

Name: ______ Class: ______ Date: ______

Chapter 5 Movie world

1 Look at this extract taken from a list of one hundred movies and write sentences using the superlative form of the adjectives in parentheses. Follow the example.

TOP 100 COMEDY MOVIES

Rank	Title	No. of Reviews
1.	Lady Bird (2017)	359
2.	BlacKkKlansman (2018)	391
3.	It Happened One Night (1934)	56
4.	Coco (2017)	317
5.	Eighth Grade (2018)	252

Available at <https://www.rottentomatoes.com/top/bestofrt/top_100_comedy_movies/>. Accessed on April 14, 2019.

a (old) *The oldest movie is* It Happened One Night.

b (good) ______

c (new) ______

d (large/number of reviews) ______

e (short/movie title) ______

f (less favorite) ______

2 Now give your opinions about movies using superlative adjectives. Follow the example.

For me, the funniest/least funny comedy movie is Lady Bird.

a great/sci-fi movie

______

b creative/animation movie

______

c boring/drama movie

______

d bad/movie genre

______

e scary/horror or thriller movie

______

3 Now read this movie review and answer the questions.

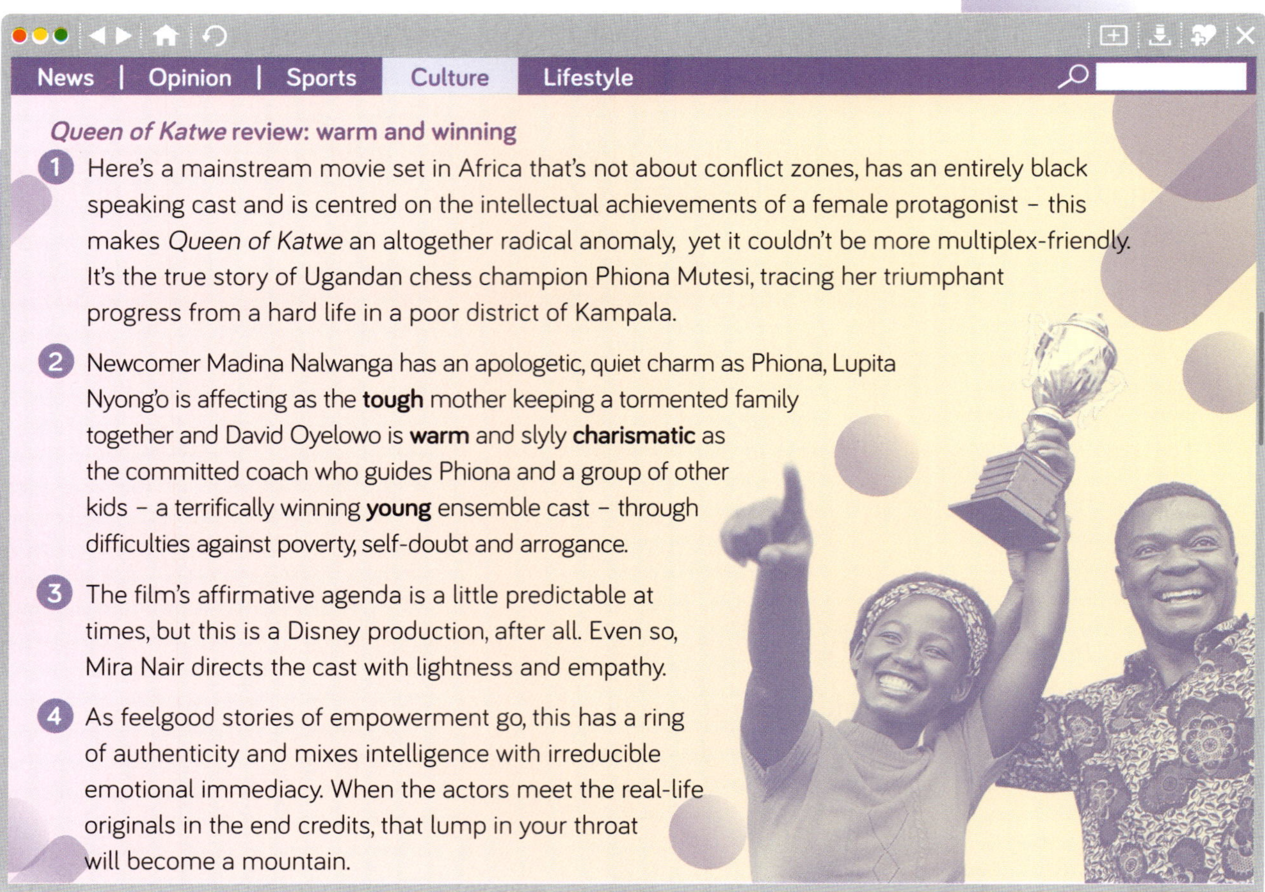

News | Opinion | Sports | Culture | Lifestyle

Queen of Katwe review: warm and winning

1 Here's a mainstream movie set in Africa that's not about conflict zones, has an entirely black speaking cast and is centred on the intellectual achievements of a female protagonist – this makes *Queen of Katwe* an altogether radical anomaly, yet it couldn't be more multiplex-friendly. It's the true story of Ugandan chess champion Phiona Mutesi, tracing her triumphant progress from a hard life in a poor district of Kampala.

2 Newcomer Madina Nalwanga has an apologetic, quiet charm as Phiona, Lupita Nyong'o is affecting as the **tough** mother keeping a tormented family together and David Oyelowo is **warm** and slyly **charismatic** as the committed coach who guides Phiona and a group of other kids – a terrifically winning **young** ensemble cast – through difficulties against poverty, self-doubt and arrogance.

3 The film's affirmative agenda is a little predictable at times, but this is a Disney production, after all. Even so, Mira Nair directs the cast with lightness and empathy.

4 As feelgood stories of empowerment go, this has a ring of authenticity and mixes intelligence with irreducible emotional immediacy. When the actors meet the real-life originals in the end credits, that lump in your throat will become a mountain.

Adapted from <https://www.theguardian.com/film/2016/oct/23/queen-of-katwe-review-chess-champion-uganda>. Accessed on April 27, 2019.

a What's the movie about?

____

b What's the movie genre? What information about the story can confirm that?

____

c Which paragraph...

- [ ] provides information about the cast?
- [ ] presents a summary of the story?
- [ ] criticizes the predictability of the movie?
- [ ] mentions the real people on which the characters are based?

d Write sentences about this movie and its characters and actors/actresses. Use the superlative form of the adjectives in bold in paragraph 2.

____

____

____

____

Name: ______________________ Class: __________ Date: __________

Chapter 6 From cover to cover

1 Complete the cartoon with the appropriate form of the verbs in parentheses. Then answer the questions.

The vegetables ______________ (sit) in the crisper for hours... days... a whole week. Then suddenly, someone ______________ (open) the drawer. A hand ______________ (reach) in, ______________ (grab) the kale and all you could hear was the sound of... a garbage disposal.

Adapted from <https://www.cartoonstock.com/cartoonview.asp?catref=smen56>. Accessed on May 10, 2019.

a According to the story told by the carrot, what were the vegetables doing?

____

b What happened suddenly?

____

c What kind of story was it?

____

d Why was the story so frightening to the vegetables?

____

2 Read these examples of microfiction. Complete them with the appropriate verbs from the box. Use the past simple or the past continuous.

answer	go	reply	see	wave

a I ______________ through some pages of my grandma's diary when I ______________ a note scribbled in a familiar handwriting: "I want to be left alone". And the diary disappeared into thin air...

b He said, "hi".

She ______________, "hello".

He asked, "when".

She ______________, "never".

He cried, "why".

She ______________ him goodbye.

3 Now answer the questions about the texts in activity 2.

a Which microfiction text did you like the most? Why?

____

b Is it possible for a diary to just disappear "into thin air"? What kinds of stories normally include events like that?

____

c How do you think the vanishing of the diary is related to the note the character saw?

____

d What did you understand from the second story? Share your ideas with a partner.

____

4 Read the fable and underline the appropriate form of the verbs.

A little Fox **played/was playing** one day when a Lion **came/was coming** roaring along. "Dear me," said the Fox, as he **hid/was hiding** behind a tree, "I never **saw/was seeing** a Lion before. What a terrible creature! His voice makes me tremble."
The next time the Fox **met/was meeting** the Lion, he was not so much afraid, but he kept a safe distance and said to himself, "I wish he would not make such a noise!"
The third time they **met/were meeting**, the Fox was not frightened at all. He **ran/was running** up to the Lion and said, "What **did/were** you **roar/roaring** about?"
And the Lion was so taken by surprise that, without saying a word, he let the Fox walk away.

Adapted from "The Fox and the Lion" in ***Æsop's Fables***.
Available at <http://www.gutenberg.org/files/49010/49010-h/49010-h.htm>. Accessed on April 30, 2019.

Workbook

Name: ______________________ Class: __________ Date: __________

Chapter 7 Communication

1 **Read these predictions and plans for the future. Complete them with *will* or *going to* and the appropriate verbs.**

One day, I __________________ a flying car.

People __________________ with their umbrellas like Mary Poppins; that's impossible!

My family and I __________________ the world. My parents have already settled everything.

I can't go anywhere because it __________________ pretty soon. Look at the sky!

2 **People often communicate using gestures. Complete the sentences with *going to* and the verbs in parentheses. Then match them to the pictures.**

b

☐ If a person does that behind his/her back, it means he/she __________________ (tell) a lie.

☐ That gesture normally indicates you __________________ (receive) an approval.

☐ When a person points to you like that, he/she __________________ probably __________________ (say) something strictly and directly.

3 Read this text about some future ideas for batteries. Complete it with the future form of the verbs in parentheses. Then write *T* (true) or *F* (false).

While smart items are growing more advanced, they're still limited by power. While chips and operating systems are becoming more efficient to save power, we only have a day or two of use on a smartphone before recharging it. Here are some battery discoveries that you ________________ (see) very soon.

We ________________ (be) able to capture energy from Wi-Fi. We ________________ (have) powered medical pills without the need for an internal battery – which is safer for the patient – and mobile devices that ________________ (not/need) to be connected to a power supply to recharge.

Devices ________________ (get) energy from their users. This ________________ (be) possible thanks to a triboelectric nanogenerator, a power-harvesting technology which captures the electric current generated through the contact of two materials.

Great minds from the University of California Irvine ________________ (make) gold nanowire batteries that ________________ (tolerate) plenty of recharging. The result ________________ (be) batteries that ________________ (not/die).

Based on <https://www.pocket-lint.com/gadgets/news/130380-future-batteries-coming-soon-charge-in-seconds-last-months-and-power-over-the-air>. Accessed on May 2, 2019.

- [ ] The text mentions two possibilities for battery recharging.
- [ ] The problem with batteries nowadays is that they don't last long before requiring to be recharged.
- [ ] Nanowire batteries will not need recharging.
- [ ] Wi-Fi-energy-capturing technology will also make medical equipment more efficient.
- [ ] We will be able to get energy from a person.

4 Read this letter Chris wrote to her friend Sue about her plans for college. Circle the appropriate options to complete the text. Then match the parts of the letter to what they indicate.

a June 17th, 2019

b Dear Sue,

c I was really glad to hear from you! How's everyone at home? I am finally writing to let you know about my plans for this early August. I **will/am going to** move to Canada as soon as my papers arrive. I've decided where I **will/am going to** live: Winnipeg! I know it's super cold there in the winter, but I have some friends who are living there at the moment and they just love it! They say the course **will/is going to** be a lot of fun and that I **will/am going to** enjoy my time in the University of Manitoba. Where **will I/am I going to** stay? Well, there is this Peruvian professor and his family who **will/are going to** rent me their attic! That **will/is going to** be super cheap and easy for me to take the bus to the university. Of course, I **will/am going to** ride a bike there, at least until winter comes.

d All the best,

e Chris

f P.S. Don't worry, I **will/am going to** let you know when I am leaving. Maybe I **will/am going to** stop by Ohio to see you guys!

- [ ] body
- [ ] closing
- [ ] greeting
- [ ] heading
- [ ] postscript
- [ ] signature

Name: ______________________ Class: __________ Date: __________

Chapter 8 What's (in the) news?

1 **Read the definition of some news vocabulary and complete the crossword puzzle.**

a An electronic traffic sign often used on roadways to give travelers information about special events.

b A heading that can be found at the top of an article or page in a newspaper or magazine.

c A screen that displays digital publicity pictures that are changed by a computer every few seconds.

d A paragraph that opens a news story.

e Person or document used in journalism to find or confirm information.

2 Read the headline. Then complete the news body with *who* or *which*.

Heroes, on screen and off, win big at MTV Movie & TV Awards show

a Superhero movie *Black Panther* made a killing at the MTV Movie & TV Awards on Monday, winning four trophies in a ceremony that also recognized gays, women and those ______________ stand up to bullying.

b *Black Panther* won best movie, best villain for Michael B. Jordan's Killmonger, and best performance and hero for star Chadwick Boseman. Boseman, ______________ plays the leader of the fictional African nation of Wakanda, gave his trophy to a man with no Hollywood connections.

c *Black Panther* actor Winston Duke thanked fans for supporting the movie, ______________ has smashed Hollywood doubts about the broader appeal of black films to become the third highest-grossing film of all time in North America.

d Actress and writer Lena Waithe, ______________ last year became the first black woman to win a screenwriting Emmy, was awarded the Trailblazer trophy.

Adapted from <https://www.reuters.com/article/us-awards-mtv/heroes-on-screen-and-off-win-big-at-mtv-movie-tv-awards-show-idUSKBN1JF0B6>. Accessed on March 21, 2019.

3 Look at these relative clauses taken from a newspaper article. Insert them in the text in order to complete it. Then answer the questions.

a which has been blamed as the root cause
b who believe that the dissemination of absolute truth
c who uses an 8-minute video to claim the Earth is flat
d which can prove devastating for babies and young children
e which believes that vaccines are harmful
f which has experienced a tremendous amount of interest online

The internet, as everyone knows, is full of some incredible nonsense. However, in the past years, some of this nonsense has been getting a lot of attention. Among the multitude of misinformation are the anti-vaccination movement, ☐, and the flat Earth theory, ☐.

Scientists are afraid that misconceptions can cause immense suffering, as is the case of the anti-vaccination movement, ☐ for recent outbreaks of measles, a viral infection ☐.

People who communicate science are, for the most part, ethical people ☐ (or, as close as we can possibly get to it) is the skeleton of a functioning, right-thinking society. This does not seem to be enough when a handsome guy ☐ comes into the picture.

The scientific community seems to be ignoring the notion that belief in pseudoscience and conspiracy theories is propelled by external pressures of fear and confusion.

Based on <https://www.theguardian.com/commentisfree/2019/apr/05/why-people-believe-the-earth-is-flat-and-we-should-listen-to-anti-vaxxers>. Accessed on April 30, 2019.

a According to the text, what are the two nonsense theories that are disseminated by the internet?

____

b In which of the sentences above the relative pronouns could be replaced by "that"?

____

Irregular verbs list

Infinitive	Past simple	Past participle	Translation
be	was/were	been	*estar; ser*
become	became	become	*tornar(-se)*
bring	brought	brought	*trazer*
build	built	built	*construir*
catch	caught	caught	*pegar*
cut	cut	cut	*cortar*
do	did	done	*fazer*
drink	drank	drunk	*beber*
fall	fell	fallen	*cair*
feel	felt	felt	*sentir*
find	found	found	*achar, encontrar*
forbid	forbade	forbidden	*proibir*
forget	forgot	forgotten	*esquecer*
get	got	got/gotten	*chegar; ficar; obter*
give	gave	given	*dar*
go	went	gone	*ir*
have	had	had	*ter*
hide	hid	hidden	*esconder, ocultar*
keep	kept	kept	*guardar; manter*
know	knew	known	*conhecer; saber*
leave	left	left	*deixar; partir*
let	let	let	*deixar, permitir*
lose	lost	lost	*perder*
make	made	made	*fazer; preparar*
meet	met	met	*encontrar(-se)*
overcome	overcame	overcome	*superar; vencer*
put	put	put	*por; colocar*
ride	rode	ridden	*andar (à cavalo, de bicicleta, de moto etc.)*
run	ran	run	*correr*
say	said	said	*dizer*
see	saw	seen	*ver*
send	sent	sent	*enviar*
speak	spoke	spoken	*falar*
spend	spent	spent	*gastar*
take	took	taken	*aceitar; levar; pegar; tomar*
teach	taught	taught	*ensinar*
tell	told	told	*contar, dizer*
think	thought	thought	*achar; pensar*
throw	threw	thrown	*atirar, lançar*
wake up	woke up	woken up	*acordar, despertar*
wear	wore	worn	*vestir, usar*
write	wrote	written	*escrever*

Language reference

Chapter 1 Future simple

Usa-se o *future simple* para:

- expressar expectativas sobre o futuro:
  *I **will have** a great job when I finish college.*
- fazer previsões para o futuro:
  *Millions of people **will not have** access to clean water.*

O *future simple* é formado pelo verbo auxiliar *will* + verbo principal no infinitivo sem a partícula *to* (*base form*).

Affirmative	Negative	Interrogative	Short answers
They **will come** tomorrow. / They**'ll come** tomorrow.	They **will not come** tomorrow. / They **won't come** tomorrow.	**Will** they **come** tomorrow?	Yes, they **will**. No, they **won't**.

Chapter 2 "Some", "any", "many", "much"

Some, *any*, *much* e *many* são quantificadores (*quantifiers*) de substantivos.

Many (muitos/muitas) é usado com substantivos contáveis no plural:

***Many** people eat more sugar than they should.*

Much (muito/muita) é usado com substantivos incontáveis; portanto, sempre no singular:

*We don't have **much** time to do our homework.*

Some (algum/alguma/alguns/algumas) pode ser usado com substantivos contáveis e incontáveis:

*We still have **some** time to finish our work.*

*They need **some** crayons to make their poster.*

Any pode ser usado com substantivos contáveis e incontáveis.

Em frases negativas, tem o sentido de nenhum/nenhuma:

*I don't have **any** friends in London.*

Em frases interrogativas, tem o sentido de algum/alguma/alguns/algumas:

*Do you need **any** help?*

Chapter 3 Present simple (review)

O *present simple*, como visto nos dois volumes anteriores, é usado para diferentes propósitos – entre eles, para expressar algo que se faz rotineiramente, descrever e identificar pessoas e expressar fatos, verdades universais ou desejos.

Na 3ª pessoa do singular (*he*/*she*/*it*), acrescenta-se *-s* ao final do verbo.

I/You/We/They ***run***. *He/She/It* ***runs***.

Se o verbo terminar em uma consoante seguida de *y*, como o verbo *to study*, retira-se o *y* e acrescenta-se *-ies*: *studies*.

Se o verbo terminar em uma vogal seguida de *y*, como o verbo *to play*, acrescenta-se apenas *-s*: *plays*.

I/You/We/They ***study***. *He/She/It* ***studies***.

I/You/We/They ***play***. *He/She/It* ***plays***.

Os verbos que terminam com *ch*, *o*, *s*, *sh*, *ss*, *x* ou *z* geralmente pedem o acréscimo de *-es* na 3ª pessoa do singular, como é o caso do verbo *to go*: *goes*.

A forma negativa se constrói com o acréscimo do verbo auxiliar *do*/*does* + a partícula *not* (ou da forma contraída *don't*/*doesn't*), seguido do infinitivo do verbo principal sem *to*:

My family ***doesn't celebrate*** *Earth Day.*

Para formar a interrogativa do *present simple*, usamos o verbo auxiliar *do*/*does* + sujeito + verbo principal na forma básica (infinitivo sem *to*):

Do *you* ***like*** *Christmas songs?*

Chapter 4 Comparative adjectives

A forma comparativa dos adjetivos é usada para comparar uma pessoa, um conceito, um lugar ou um objeto em relação a outro.

O comparativo dos adjetivos de duas sílabas ou mais é feito colocando-se *more* antes do adjetivo e *than* após ele:

A car is ***more expensive than*** *a bicycle.*

O comparativo dos adjetivos de uma sílaba é feito acrescentando-se *-er* ao final do adjetivo, seguido da palavra *than*:

A car is ***faster than*** *a bicycle.*

Se o adjetivo utilizado na forma comparativa terminar em consoante-vogal-consoante (c-v-c), duplica-se a última consoante e acrescenta-se *-er*: *bigger*.

Alguns adjetivos são irregulares e não seguem as regras apresentadas, pois têm formas próprias:

good – better

bad – worse

far – farther/further

Chapter 5 Superlative adjectives

O grau superlativo dos adjetivos é usado para comparar uma pessoa, um conceito, um lugar ou um objeto a um grupo de pessoas, conceitos, lugares ou objetos:

*São Paulo is **the largest** city in Brazil.*

O superlativo dos adjetivos de duas sílabas ou mais é feito acrescentando-se *the most* antes do adjetivo:

*Lima is **the most important** city in Peru.*

O superlativo dos adjetivos de uma sílaba é feito acrescentando-se *the* antes do adjetivo e *-est* ao final dele:

*São Vicente is **the oldest** city in Brazil.*

Se o adjetivo utilizado na forma superlativa terminar em consoante-vogal-consoante (c-v-c), duplica-se a última consoante e acrescenta-se *-est*: *biggest*.

Alguns adjetivos são irregulares e não seguem as regras apresentadas, pois têm formas próprias:

good – best

bad – worst

far – farthest/furthest

Chapter 6 Past simple X past continuous (review)

Past simple	
Utilizado para falar sobre ações que começaram e terminaram em um momento determinado do passado.	Affirmative: *He **illustrated** the book that she **wrote**.* Negative: *They **did not read** that book.* Interrogative: ***Did** you **write** this book? It's great!*

Past continuous	
Utilizado para falar sobre uma ação que estava em progresso em um período específico do passado. Utilizado para falar sobre um evento que estava acontecendo em um período do passado quando ocorreu outro evento, também no passado. Nesse caso, utilizamos *when* e a ação que ocorreu durante a primeira fica no *past simple*. *I **was sleeping** when my father **arrived**.* Obs.: Para falar sobre duas ações que estavam acontecendo simultaneamente no passado, utiliza-se *while*. Nesse caso, ambas as ações ficam no *past continuous*. *While I **was reading** a romance, my brother **was reading** a horror book.*	Affirmative: *She **was writing** a short story yesterday night.* Negative: *The girls **were not paying** attention to what the teacher **was reading**.* Interrogative: *What **were** you **reading**?* 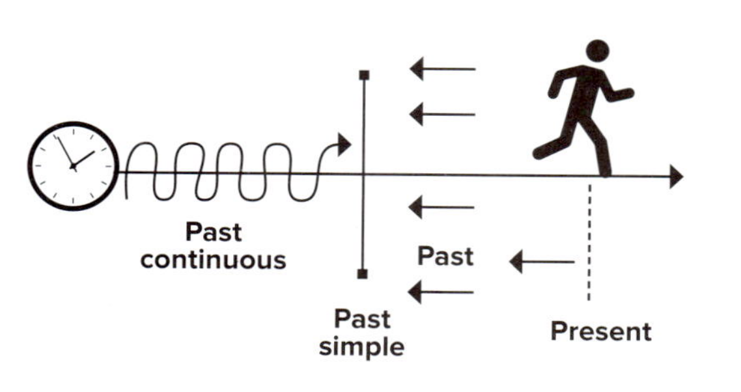

Chapter 7 "Will" X "going to"

Futuro	
Previsões	**Planos e intenções**
Will/Going to	***Going to***
Em situações em que há evidências de que algo acontecerá no futuro como resultado de algo que se vê ou se sabe no presente, utiliza-se *going to*. *Look at those clouds in the sky! It* ***is going to rain*** *soon.* Em situações de surpresa, quando algo que não se estava planejando acontece, é comum a utilização de *will* para descrever a ação que se decide realizar. – *The phone is ringing.* – ***I'll get*** *it.*	*My sister told me she* ***is going to buy*** *a car.* *I* ***am going to watch*** *a movie tomorrow. Do you want to go with me? I've already bought the tickets.*

Estrutura	
Will	***Going to***
Affirmative: *Be careful! It* ***will hurt*** *you.* Interrogative: ***Will*** *screens* ***disappear*** *in five years?* Negative: *In my opinion, people* ***will not stop*** *using their phones.*	Affirmative: *She* ***is going to have*** *a baby.* Interrogative: ***Is*** *he* ***going to come*** *to the party?* Negative: *We* ***are not going to have*** *classes this Saturday.*

Chapter 8 Relative pronouns

Os pronomes relativos *who*, *which*, *that* e *whose* são empregados para fazer referência a um elemento já mencionado na frase, identificando-o e acrescentando alguma informação sobre ele ou indicando uma relação de posse/pertencimento.

Em linhas gerais, os pronomes relativos podem ser resumidos da seguinte forma:

Pronome	A que se refere?	Pode ser omitido?	Pode ser substituído por *that*?
who	pessoas	Sim, quando restringe sobre quem se fala e é seguido de um pronome ou substantivo.	Sim, quando restringe sobre quem se fala.
which	objetos, animais, lugares, substantivos abstratos etc.	Sim, quando restringe sobre o que se fala e é seguido de um pronome ou substantivo.	Sim, quando restringe sobre o que se fala.
whose	posse/pertencimento de pessoas, objetos, animais, lugares, substantivos abstratos etc.	Não.	Não.
that	pessoas, objetos, animais, lugares, substantivos abstratos etc.	Sim, quando restringe sobre quem/o que se fala e é seguido de um pronome ou substantivo.	—

Interdisciplinary project

Culture of the English-speaking countries

Presentation

Vamos mergulhar na diversidade cultural dos países de língua inglesa?

Procedures

Part I (Geography, English and Arts)

Objective: learn (or review) what countries have English as either a native or an official language. Find out what these countries have produced in terms of art and culture.

Resources: atlas (physical or digital), encyclopedia (physical or digital), internet.

Instructions

a Descubram (ou revisem) quais são os países do mundo que têm o inglês como língua nativa ou língua oficial. Considerem países dos cinco continentes: África, América, Ásia, Europa, Oceania.

b Formem grupos. Com base nos países levantados, criem uma lista daqueles com os quais seu grupo irá trabalhar. Certifiquem-se de que, em sua lista, sejam contemplados países dos cinco continentes e de que, na medida do possível, eles sejam diferentes daqueles escolhidos por outros grupos.

c Criem uma ficha para cada um dos países atribuídos a seu grupo. Em cada ficha, listem algumas das principais manifestações artístico-culturais produzidas no país em questão, por exemplo: artes plásticas (pintura, arquitetura, escultura etc.), visuais (vídeo, cinema, fotografia etc.), literatura (romance, poema, conto etc.), música (folclórica, clássica, popular etc.), cinema (ficção, documentário, drama etc.), dança (folclórica, clássica, urbana etc.), festividades (nacionais, regionais, locais etc.).

Analysis

Analisem as informações registradas nas fichas dos países. Há manifestações artístico-culturais exclusivas de algum dos países? Quais são observáveis em todos os países? Há alguma que não esteja presente em nenhum dos países?

Reflections

Na sua visão, o que pode explicar uma quantidade maior de manifestações artístico-culturais em um determinado país de língua inglesa? Por que algumas delas são observáveis em todos os países? Tome nota de suas ideias.

Part II (History and Geography)

Objective: understand why some English-speaking countries are culturally richer than others in one or more aspects. Understand why certain types of artistic and cultural production are present in one place and absent in others.

Resources: History books, internet.

Instructions

a Pesquisem a história de cada um dos países em estudo. Procurem saber, por exemplo, se seu histórico é de país colonizador ou colonizado, se foi marcado pela escravidão, se já houve restrição à liberdade de expressão em seu território, como sua economia se desenvolveu, que outras línguas além do inglês constituem sua história etc.

Analysis

Analisem a relação entre a produção artístico-cultural de cada país e a sua história, sua economia, seu regime político, suas condições geográficas etc. É possível concluir que um país é culturalmente mais rico que outro em decorrência de algum desses fatores? É possível relacionar o tipo de arte e cultura de cada país com algum desses fatores?

b Analisem a geografia física de cada país (relevo, vegetação, clima) e investiguem de que maneira a sua população interage com o ambiente e ocupa espaços rurais e urbanos.

c Procurem descobrir se as características da produção artístico-cultural de cada um dos países pesquisados estão relacionadas com as informações históricas e geográficas levantadas.

Reflections

Discutam as seguintes questões: 1. O que foi possível concluir até aqui com sua pesquisa? Considere, por exemplo, as diferenças observadas entre a produção artístico-cultural dos diferentes países, a despeito de terem o mesmo idioma como língua nativa ou oficial. 2. Há algum dado que tenha surpreendido o grupo?

Part III (Math)

Objective: investigate the presence of English in your community.

Resources: data collected in field trips, internet.

Instructions

a Coletem o maior número possível de amostras da produção artístico-cultural dos países pesquisados por seu grupo. Dada a grande quantidade de conteúdo disponível na internet, procurem selecionar algumas amostras com base nesse suporte. Considerem, também, livros, filmes em DVD, catálogos turísticos etc.

b Selecionem aspectos específicos dessas amostras que sejam representativos das características dos países que o grupo levantou na Parte II do projeto. Por exemplo, verifique se um país que tenha sido colonizado por outro apresenta, em sua produção artístico-cultural, manifestações relacionadas a resistência, lutas, superação etc.

Analysis

Analisem o material selecionado com base em questões como: 1. De que maneira expressões como a música, a dança, a literatura, a pintura etc. dos países pesquisados podem ser interpretadas em função de aspectos culturais e históricos? 2. O que difere um país de outro, tomando como base fatores como localização geográfica e história? 3. Há elementos em comum observados em países situados no mesmo continente?

Reflections

Discutam: 1. Vocês se depararam com outros dados muito diferentes daqueles que já haviam sido constatados nas Partes I e II do projeto? 2. Houve dificuldade ao tentar interpretar as expressões artísticas de um determinado país em função de seus aspectos culturais? Por quê? 3. Vocês diriam que sua visão em relação à grande diversidade das manifestações artístico-culturais

Sharing knowledge

Preparem agora uma apresentação das informações que mais chamaram a sua atenção em suas descobertas. Considerem compartilhar suas descobertas com outras turmas e, se possível, com pessoas de fora da comunidade escolar.

Instructions

a Conversem com os/as professores/professoras envolvidos/as na realização de seu projeto. Peçam-lhes que revisem as informações do grupo e façam os ajustes que julgarem necessários. Essa validação é importante, principalmente, para garantir que o material compartilhado não contenha incorreções.

b Com base no *feedback*, preparem a versão final da apresentação. Decidam como fazer a exibição das amostras de produção artístico-culturais dos países pesquisados.

Presentation

Apresentem as descobertas de suas pesquisas para outras turmas ou para pessoas de fora da comunidade escolar. Decidam se esses públicos podem participar de um mesmo evento ou se seria recomendável estipular momentos diferentes para cada um.

Assessment

Avaliem, em conjunto com todos/as os/as participantes do projeto, os conhecimentos e reflexões obtidos com esse trabalho e de que maneira esse aprendizado poderá ser útil na sequência de seus estudos. Considerem, também, a possibilidade de elaborar um relatório do projeto, como um registro a ser mobilizado no projeto do ano seguinte.

Transcripts

Chapter 1

Track 2 – Page 17

Well, luckily, nowadays you don't have to be a psychic to predict the future. Sometimes it's enough just to analyze the present. Here are the events that are planned to happen or will probably happen by the year 2050.

Track 3 – Page 17

In the year 2025, the population of Earth will reach eight billion people. What's more: people's life expectancy will get longer and there will be 50 times more centenarians. It will be possible to charge electronic devices using Wi-Fi.

In the year 2028, Venice may become uninhabitable. It doesn't mean that the city will be completely under water. It might happen, but not before the year 2100. However, there are concerns that the water level in the Venetian Lagoon will raise so much that it will be impossible to live in the houses.

In the year 2030, the area of the Arctic ice sheet will be extremely small. According to some estimations, the Arctic Ocean will melt completely in the summer period before the end of the 21st century.

And in the year 2050, fifty percent of the world's population will suffer from short-sightedness. Hey, don't we have that now? So, which of these predicted future events will you look forward to?

Extracts from the audio available at <https://www.youtube.com/watch?v=Cip3LmqQ7Y0>. Accessed on May 13, 2019.

Chapter 2

Track 4 – Page 29

Speaker 1: I was diagnosed with ADHD around second grade and when I was diagnosed, we started getting different medications for it until I found the right one. A challenge is definitely being able to focus even well on my medicine. I have to do a lot to maintain focus and to keep, like, stay on tasks and stay on track.

Speaker 2: I've been put on medication so that my asthma acts up less frequently. Every morning when I wake up, I have to take my inhaler. And every evening before I go to bed, I have to take my inhaler. Any opportunity I get, I go outside and start running up and down the street just so I can work my legs out.

Speaker 3: I've had diabetes for five years now and I'm hoping there's a cure. I've really always been used to getting shots and stuff like that because I'm always in the hospital. Don't ask me why, but it's like a thing, I'm always getting sick and I'm the only one in the house that usually gets sick. I eat healthy, like, before I ever had diabetes I always ate healthy. I don't really drink soda. My parents always buy me water.

Speaker 4: I have depression, so I take pills and stuff to help me keep myself happy. Some things that have helped with my depression, obviously the medication, but my friends have been a big part of helping, because it's always nice, because I feel more open with my friends to talk about stuff that I probably wouldn't talk with my parents about. It depends on the day for exercising. I sometimes I have to push myself, but in the end it always... I always end up feeling better.

Extract from the audio available at <https://www.youtube.com/watch?v=c5C5WptbBbY>. Accessed on May 13, 2019.

Chapter 3

Track 5 – Page 39

1

[Excerpt of traditional square dance.]

Extract from the audio available at <https://www.youtube.com/watch?v=Upu1l3eLid4&list=RDUpu1l3eLid4&t=60>. Accessed on May 13, 2019.

2

[Excerpt of Irish step dance.]

Extract from the audio available at <https://www.youtube.com/watch?v=HgGAzBDE454>. Accessed on May 13, 2019.

3

[Excerpt of Australian aboriginal dance.]

Extract from the audio available at <https://www.youtube.com/watch?v=QIKByvQN0Ho>. Accessed on May 13, 2019.

Track 6 – Page 39

Hey, there. I'll make a quick video on the history of traditional Irish music.

Track 7 – Pages 39-40

Hey, there. I'll make a quick video on the history of traditional Irish music. It all started when the Celts came to Ireland around the first century AD. They brought with them a strong sense of tradition, culture and music from Eastern Europe, which they had been settled in since about 500 BC. In Eastern Europe, they were influenced heavily by the cultures in Asia as well as in North Africa. The most popular traditional Irish instrument is the harp and there is evidence to suggest that the harp started its life in Egypt. Other instruments that they would use would be the bodhrán, which is an Irish frame drum. They would use the fiddle, which is exactly the same as our modern violin, except musicologists use the term "fiddle" when referring to folk music. They would use the tin whistle, which is a wind instrument, kind of shaped like a recorder. It's got six holes for you to cover with your fingers, a more shrill sound than the flute, which is gonna have a warmer sound. They usually use wooden flutes and most traditional Irish bands today are supposed to use a wooden flute as opposed to the modern metal ones. Aside from instruments, the voice was a huge part in traditional Irish music. Like much folk music from around the world, Irish music was very much about storytelling and having the voice with lyrics and words would obviously help telling a story. So that's a very brief history on Irish music.

Extracts from the audio available at <https://www.youtube.com/watch?v=Pt60LrWPOU8>. Accessed on May 13, 2019.

Track 8 – Page 55

Part 1

1. **Narrator:** This painting is called Christina's World. The woman on the ground is Christina. She was a friend and neighbor of the artist, Andrew Wyeth. She lived in that house off in the distance—can you see her laundry hanging on the clothes line outside?

Look at the field surrounding Christina—this land was her farm. The artist painted each blade of grass, one at a time, filling almost the entire painting.

2. **Narrator:** Take a few steps back from this painting so you can see the whole thing. Now imagine jumping into the scene.

You're trudging through the deep, dark jungle! Carefully, you part the tall ferns in the center.

Aaah! Lions! One of them, with fierce, yellow eyes is staring right at you. Quick—roar back at him!

In the jungle you meet all sorts of beasts. Can you find one that might sound like this?

Yep, there's a bird perched high on a branch of the orange tree... And another up at the top on the left, flapping off with its yellow wings...

How about this critter?

Did you find the elephant, behind the orange tree? Wave your "trunk" and bellow back at him!

Track 9 – Page 55

Part 2

1. **Kid:** But why is she on the ground, all alone?

Narrator: Christina wasn't able to walk. But she didn't want any help getting around, so instead of using crutches or a wheelchair, she crawled on the ground. The artist thought she was brave and strong to live that way, and he made this painting to honor her.

We can't see Christina's face—what do you think her expression might be? Make that expression yourself!

2. **Narrator:** Okay, what else would you find in a jungle? How 'bout a young woman relaxing on a velvet sofa? Whoa, wait a minute—there's something strange about this place. That's because you've entered into a dream!

The Dream is what the artist Henri Rousseau called his painting.

Rousseau never actually went to the jungle. In fact, he never traveled far from his home in Paris! He got ideas for paintings like this one from visiting zoos, city gardens, and museums and from his "dreamy" imagination.

Extracts from the audios available at <https://www.moma.org/audio/playlist/2/342>; <https://www.moma.org/audio/playlist/2/143>. Accessed on May 13, 2019.

Chapter 5

Track 10 – Page 69

Voice over: Welcome to "Teen Talk", where we learn what Marysville high school students are thinking.

Hostess: Hello, and welcome to "Teen Talk" on M6, your hometown station. Today we will ask high school students about movies. What is your favorite movie ever made?

Boy 1: Oh, my favorite movie of all time would have to be Napoleon Dynamite because it's a... just a classic, funny movie.

Boy 2: My favorite movie ever made is Driving Miss Daisy because I think the storyline is amazing and it has a lot of meaning to it.

Boy 3: My favorite movie ever made was definitely The Lion King. It was a big part of my childhood and I loved every moment of it.

Hostess: What do you think the better movie series is, Harry Potter or Star Wars?

Boy 1: I have to say Star Wars because I've never really been a fan of Harry Potter.

Boy 2: A better movie series would be Star Wars. I think there's a lot more action in those ones rather than Harry Potter.

Boy 3: I think the better series is Harry Potter because I've seen all the Harry Potter movies and I've yet to see any Star Wars movies.

Boy 4: Star Wars, every possible way. It's better.

Boy 5: Um... I have to say Star Wars is the better one, because it's, like, more widely known and the effects in its day were the best.

Boy 6: Star Wars is by far the better movie series and it has more action and it's just more entertaining to watch.

Hostess: I'm McKenzie Guzzo and this has been "Teen Talk" on M6, your hometown station.

Extract from the audio available at <https://www.youtube.com/watch?v=C4ylaiW23ko>. Accessed on May 13, 2019.

Chapter 6

Track 11 – Page 81

When Jane Eyre was initially published, the many admirers of the novel did not know, though some suspected, that it had been written by a woman. Charlotte Brontë, who wrote the novel under the gender-ambiguous pseudonym, Currer Bell, knew firsthand of the challenges faced by an independent, intellectual woman who lacked social station in Victorian English society.

Track 12 – Page 81

Jane Eyre begins with 10-year-old Jane living a life of torment with her Aunt Reed and cousins John, Eliza and Georgiana. One day, the apothecary, Mr. Lloyd, comes and suggests she go to school. A few months later, Jane goes to Lowood Institute, a poor orphan school. She makes friends with Helen Burns, who teaches Jane to control her passions. After a typhus epidemic passes through the school, Helen dies, and a new administration comes in.

Track 13 – Page 81

Jane finishes school and teaches there for two years before being offered a governess position. She takes the post and moves to Thornfield, where she falls in love with Mr. Rochester. One night she saves his life when she puts out a fire in his room, but remains unsure who set it. Mr. Rochester tells her that a servant, Grace Poole, was responsible. Jane is called back to her aunt's estate because Aunt Reed is dying.

On her death bed, Aunt Reed tells Jane she does not regret the way she treated her. She reveals that her uncle, John Eyre, has been trying to find Jane to adopt her and leave her his fortune. Mrs. Reed told him that Jane was dead. When Jane returns to Thornfield, Mr. Rochester reveals that he is secretly in love with her. He asks her to marry him. Jane accepts and they go to get married. However, the marriage is interrupted by a lawyer, Mr. Briggs, who claims Rochester is already married. Rochester admits that he married a mad woman and brings everyone back to Thornfield to reveal his wife Bertha living on the third floor, cared for by Grace Poole. Jane forgives him, but flees Thornfield and ends up destitute.

Extracts from the audio available at <https://www.youtube.com/watch?v=FsGS1WTf8ag>. Accessed on May 13, 2019.

Track 14 – Page 94

It's well known that some gestures mean different things in different parts of the world.

Track 15 – Pages 94-95

Gesture a: In some places such as Britain, this means everything's OK. And in still other places, such as Japan, it means money.

Gesture b: In Italy, they might make this sign to emphasize a point, while in Jordan it can mean "wait a second".

Gesture c: Some places have more or less unique gestures. In Russia, to say "you're making things too complicated", you scratch your ear by going around the back of your head.

Track 16 – Page 95

Among the most common and probably oldest gestures are nodding for "yes" and shaking the head for "no". But even this isn't universal. Bulgarians are famous for shaking the head to mean "yes" and nodding with a click of the tongue to mean "no".

Extracts from the audio available at <https://www.youtube.com/watch?v=qCo3wSGYRbQ>. Accessed on May 13, 2019.

Track 17 – Pages 106-107

Reporter: The world is drowning in plastic waste. It's clogging the oceans and choking wildlife, which is why Science whiz Angelina Arora invented a solution.

Angelina Arora: I created a plastic. It's a biodegradable plastic. It starts to break down within five days and it completely breaks down in 33 days.

Reporter: Supervised by her teacher, Angelina first started experimenting in 2016, using corn starch to develop a prize-winning biodegradable plastic. Unfortunately, it broke down when exposed to water. But a spark had been ignited in this budding scientist.

Ajsa Mahmic: She's dedicated. She has a passion to find solutions to a problem. She's resilient and hard-working.

Reporter: Then last year Angelina had an epiphany.

Angelina: I was looking at prawns and I saw that they were plasticky, so I wondered what makes them look like plastic.

Reporter: Turns out prawn shells contain a special carbohydrate called chitin. Angelina's bioplastic is created by isolating that carbohydrate and combining it with fibroin, the sticky material in spiders' webs and silk cocoons. Together, the raw materials create a flexible strong substance that acts just like plastic, but with none of the harmful side effects.

Angelina: Australia is a massive producer of sea food waste and all that waste is going into landfill. So I'm taking them out of landfill as well as putting them to a good purpose. Age shouldn't be a limit to invention and discovery. It can be young people wanting to go out of their comfort zone, go outside of the classroom, and create and innovate and come up with ideas that potentially change the world.

Extracts from the audio available at <https://vimeo.com/275093225>. Accessed on May 13, 2019.

Glossary

CHAPTER 1

A
account: conta
advance: avanço
advertise: divulgar, promover
anymore: não mais
arrow: seta
as long as: enquanto
automated/autonomous car: veículo autônomo
available: disponível

B
beat: derrotar
better: melhor
bot: programa de computador
brain: cérebro
build: construir, fazer

C
careful: cuidadoso/a
charge: recarregar
chess: xadrez
commute: ir ao/à e voltar do/a trabalho/escola
crop: colheita, cultura agrícola, safra

D
develop: desenvolver
discovery: descoberta
disease: doença
driver: motorista

E
Earth: Terra
else: mais (algo), outro
enough: suficiente
excited: empolgado/a

F
fade away: desaparecer
feature: característica
fewer: menos
floppy disk: disquete

G
garbage: lixo
grain: cereal, grão
great: grande; ótimo/a

H
hold: guardar
housing: habitação

I
ice sheet: manto de gelo
illness: doença
increasing: crescente

K
kind: tipo; bondoso/a

L
layperson: leigo/a
less: menos
lightning: raio, relâmpago
likely: provável; provavelmente
lives: vidas (pl. de *life*)
look forward to: esperar ansiosamente

M
made of: feito/a de
mean: significar
means: meio, recurso
mobile: móvel
Moon: Lua

N
near: próximo/a
nowadays: atualmente, hoje em dia

O
other: outro/a

P
pay: pagar
powerful: potente
printer: impressora
psychic: médium

R
rehearse: ensaiar
researcher: pesquisador/a
rise: aumentar, subir

S
show: mostrar
social divide: desigualdade social
sustainable: sustentável

T
take a look: dar uma olhada
tell: dizer
time: prazo; tempo; vez
tool: ferramenta
try: tentar
turn out: acabar sendo

U
uninhabitable: inabitável

V
vacation: férias

W
wind: eólico/a, relativo ao vento

Y
year: ano

CHAPTER 2

A
absence: ausência
ADHD (attention deficit hyperactivity disorder): transtorno do déficit de atenção com hiperatividade
anger: raiva
any: algum/a (em perguntas); nenhum/a (em frases negativas); todos/as os/as (em frases afirmativas)
apply: aplicar-se
awesome: incrível

B
blush: corar
body: corpo; corporal

C
cell: célula
cold: resfriado; frio/a
countable: contável
cue: dica

D
dead: morto/a
digress: divagar

E
easily: facilmente
eating disorder: distúrbio alimentar
essay: dissertação, texto
everywhere: em todo lugar

F
fit: em forma; servir

G
guilty: culpado/a

I
inhaler: inalador
inside: dentro

J
judge: julgar

K
keep: manter-se

L
lack: carecer de, não ter; falta
laxative: laxante
low: baixo/a, pouco/a

M
make sure: certificar-se
makeup: maquiagem
many: muitos/as
mess up: atrapalhar-se, errar
mild: suave
mistake: erro
moody: temperamental

O
overcome: superar
overeat: comer exageradamente
oversleep: dormir até perder a hora

P
pain: dor
physician: médico/a
pimple: espinha (acne)
print media: mídia impressa

R
ratio: proporção
redness: vermelhidão

S
safe: seguro/a
salicylic acid: ácido salicílico
scared: com medo
shape: forma
sit down: sentar-se
skin: pele
soap: sabonete
stage: palco
stranger: desconhecido/a, estranho/a
sunscreen: protetor solar
sweaty: suado/a
swelling: inchaço

T
throat: garganta
tighten: contrair-se
trapped: preso/a
trigger: gatilho
trouble: dificuldade
trust: confiar
twist: torcer

U
upset: chateado/a

W
wake up: acordar
warm: morno/a
wash: lavar
worry: preocupação; preocupar-se
written: escrito/a

CHAPTER 3

A
among: entre (vários)

B
blood: sangue
bottle: garrafa
brief: breve
burning: queimadura

C
cheap: barato/a
Chemistry: Química
cross legs: cruzar as pernas
crowd: multidão

D
decay: decompor-se
deep: intenso; profundo
douse: encharcar

E
environment: meio ambiente

F
face: rosto; encarar
fall: cair
fold arms: cruzar os braços
folk: folclórico/a
folks: pessoal (coloquial)
forehead: testa
fortress: fortaleza

G
gift: presente

H
harm: prejudicar
hazardous: perigoso/a
hip: quadril

I
inhabited: habitado/a
iron: ferro

J
jewelry: joias

L
let go: abandonar

M
married: casado/a
mile: milha
mirror: espelho

N
nephew: sobrinho

O
obey: obedecer

P
parade: desfile, parada
pocket: bolso
price: preço

R
report: relatório
root: raiz

S
silk: seda
smile: sorrir
spread: difusão, propagação; difundir, propagar
spring: primavera
square dance: dança de quadrilha

T
take: levar
though: embora
throw: jogar
tie: amarrar
trash: lixo

U
uncomfortable: desconfortável
unsure: incerto/a, inseguro/a
usage: uso

V
visual prop: suporte visual

W
windmill: moinho de vento
wrist: pulso

CHAPTER 4

A
appreciate: apreciar
approach: aproximar-se
artwork: obra de arte
at least: pelo menos

B
bored: entediado/a
bright: brilhante, forte, viva (cor)

C
cardboard: papelão
catch: capturar
challenging: desafiador/a
craft: artesanato
crawl: rastejar
crutch: muleta
cut: cortar

D
displaced: deslocado/a

E
elephant seal: elefante-marinho

F
force away: expulsar
frog: sapo

G
ground: chão
guide: guia; guiar

H
half: meio/a, metade

J
jungle: selva

L
light: claro/a
line up: formar uma fila

P
portray: retratar
poverty: pobreza

R
refugee: refugiado/a
revenge: vingança

S
scenery: cenário
seem: parecer
self-portrait: autorretrato
sensitive: compreensivo/a
shocking: chocante
suffer: sofrer
surrounded: cercado/a

T
take pictures: tirar fotos
thinker: pensador/a

V
visually impaired: deficiente visual

W
wave: acenar
weird: estranho/a
wheelchair: cadeira de rodas

CHAPTER 5

A
acceptance: aceitação

B
be born: nascer
blend in: misturar-se
boring: chato/a
box office: bilheteria

C
cast: elenco
clapperboard: claquete
closed caption: legenda oculta

D
deal: lidar

E
elementary school: ensino fundamental
encompass: englobar
enjoy: gostar
evaluation: avaliação

G
genre: gênero
glad: feliz, satisfeito/a

H
heartbreaking: de partir o coração
heartwarming: comovente
hostess: anfitriã

J
journey: jornada

M
mainstream: convencional

O
ordinary: comum

P
parental guidance: orientação dos pais

R
rating: nota
record: relato
respectful: respeitoso/a
review: resenha
rotten: estragado/a
runtime: duração

S
score: pontuação
shy away: fugir
snoozer (coloquial): algo maçante, que dá sono
soppiness: sentimentalismo
stand out: destacar-se
struggle: lutar
subpar: abaixo da média

T
thriller: suspense
transcribe: transcrever
translate: traduzir

U
uplifting: edificante, inspirador

V
valuable: valioso/a

W
winsome: cativante

CHAPTER 6

A
accomplishment: realização
accursed: amaldiçoado/a

B
bedchamber (arcaico): quarto
behold: contemplar
bone: osso
booklet: livreto
breathe: respirar

C
cheer up: alegrar, animar
cover: capa
coverage: cobertura
crash: colisão
currently: atualmente

D
deadline: prazo
die: morrer
dreary: feio/a, melancólico/a (clima)
dull: opaco/a

E
eager: ávido/a, impaciente
endue: dotar, receber como característica
expensively: de forma cara

F
fair: feira
flesh: carne (humana)
fulfill: cumprir, realizar

H
hateful: odioso/a
hurt: machucar

L
lawyer: advogado/a
lay: estava deitado/a, jazia
limb: membro (do corpo)
literary piece: obra literária
loathsome: repugnante

N
nearly: quase

P
pleased: satisfeito/a
put out: apagar

R
revengeful: vingativo/a
reward: recompensa
rhythm: ritmo
rush out: sair correndo

S
set: determinar
shatter: destruir, estilhaçar
sketchbook: caderno de desenho
sole: único/a
spark: faísca
suddenly: de repente
suitable: apropriado/a

V
vanish: desaparecer
vow: jurar

W
wound: ferida

CHAPTER 7

A
achieve: alcançar
advise: aconselhar
as soon as: assim que

B
busy line: linha ocupada

C
closing: encerramento
concise: conciso/a

G
greeting: cumprimento, saudação

H
heading: cabeçalho

I
inland: interior, longe da costa

L
landlord: senhorio, proprietário/a
lean: esguio/a, magro/a
low battery: bateria fraca

M
mail: correio; correspondência
mostly: principalmente

N
nod: acenar com a cabeça para cima e para baixo
note: anotação; observação; recado

P
poor signal: sinal fraco
prancing: saltitante

R
reach: alcançar, chegar a
retreat: recuar

S
sea: mar
shake: acenar para um lado e para o outro
signature: assinatura
slow: lento/a
summon: convocar; juntar

T
tongue: língua

W
waterway: rio ou canal navegável
woods: bosque

CHAPTER 8

A
addictive: viciante

B
billboard: *outdoor* (anglicismo)
breaking news: notícia de última hora
broadcast: transmitir

C
can't stand: não suportar
cocoon: casulo
concerned: preocupado/a
corn starch: amido de milho

D
deserve: merecer
display: exibir

E
endangered: em perigo de extinção

F
forecast: previsão

H
harmful: nocivo/a, prejudicial

K
keep up with: acompanhar

L
landfill: aterro
lead: introdução, lide
lecturer: professor/a universitário/a

N
noise: barulho

P
prawn: camarão

R
rebut: refutar
road: estrada

S
seal: foca
shell: carapaça, casca; concha
shot: chance
sticky: grudento/a, pegajoso/a

T
take over: dominar, tomar conta
trustworthy: confiável

U
unreliable: não confiável

V
variable: variável

W
web: teia

Learning more

Capítulo 1

Cosmos: A Spacetime Odyssey

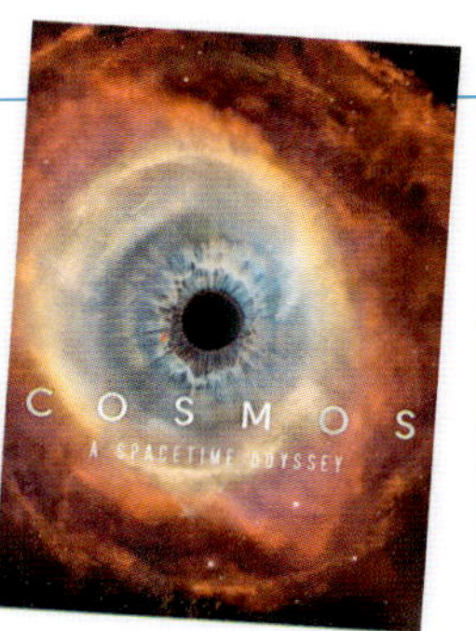

Produzido por Seth MacFarlane, Ann Druyan, Brannon Braga e Mitchell Cannold.
Estados Unidos: Cosmos Studios, 2014.

A série *Cosmos* explica como o nosso planeta se formou, como está hoje e como poderá ser no futuro. Apresentado pelo astrofísico Neil deGrasse Tyson, o programa tem fundamentação científica confiável. O objetivo é tentar responder às perguntas que a maioria das pessoas já se fez alguma vez na vida: de onde viemos e para onde vamos? Talvez ainda não tenhamos tecnologia suficiente para dar respostas definitivas quanto a isso, mas o programa cita possibilidades.

Capítulo 2

So Much to Tell You

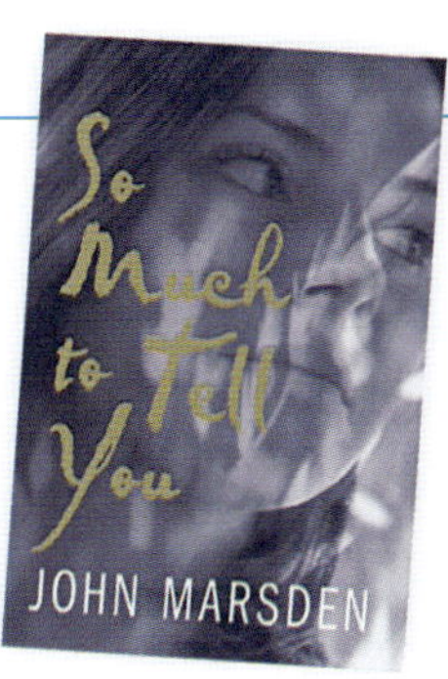

Escrito por John Marsden.
Sydney: Hachette Australia, 2012.

No enredo desse livro, originalmente publicado em 1987, Marina, após ter o rosto marcado por uma agressão paterna, passa a se retrair e ter grande dificuldade de se expressar. Sua mãe a matricula em um colégio interno na intenção de ajudá-la a se recuperar do trauma vivenciado. Lá, a garota começa a escrever em um diário pessoal e aos poucos consegue aprender a lidar com seus problemas e situações cotidianas.

Capítulo 3

Coco

Dirigido por Lee Unkrich.
Estados Unidos: Pixar Animation Studios, 2017.

Miguel, um garoto de 12 anos, sonha em ser músico. Para participar de uma competição de talentos, ele decide usar o violão que está guardado em um mausoléu. No entanto, por profanar um túmulo, acaba sendo levado para o mundo dos mortos, de onde só poderá sair se for abençoado por um ente já falecido. A animação introduz elementos da cultura mexicana relacionados ao Dia dos Mortos.

Capítulo 4

The National Gallery, London

Mantendo um dos maiores acervos de obras de arte do mundo, a Galeria Nacional de Londres é uma das poucas que oferece entrada gratuita para a coleção principal. O *site* oficial do museu conta com passeios virtuais controlados pelo visitante, que pode "caminhar" pelas salas da galeria de arte e ler as descrições das obras que mais o interessarem.

Capítulo 5

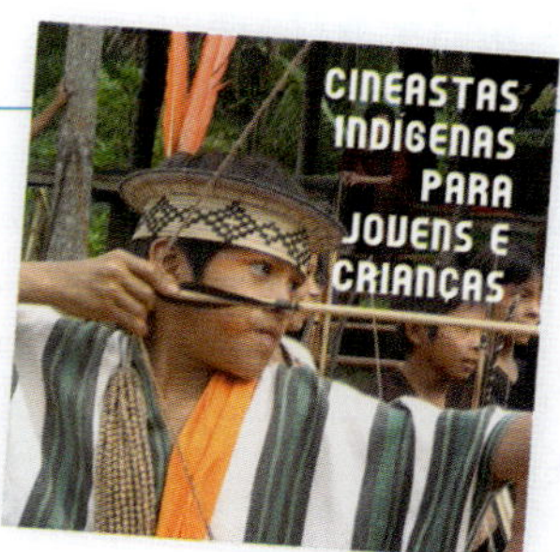

Cineastas Indígenas para Jovens e Crianças

Escrito por Ana Carvalho Ziller de Araujo, Rita Carelli e Vincent Carelli.
Olinda: Vídeo nas Aldeias, 2010.

Este livro-vídeo, amparado pela “Convenção sobre a proteção e promoção da diversidade das expressões culturais” da UNESCO, apresenta uma coletânea de informações e indicações de filmes realizados junto com os povos indígenas brasileiros Wajãpi, Ikpeng, Panará, Ashaninka, Mbya-Guarani e Kisêdjê. Conhecer sua história e cultura é o primeiro passo para respeitá-las.

Capítulo 6

Projeto Gutenberg

O projeto Gutenberg, um esforço voluntário do escritor estadunidense Michael S. Hart, foi uma enorme inovação. Fundado em 1971, permanece sendo um dos maiores acervos digitais de obras literárias do mundo, oferecendo acesso gratuito a mais de 57 mil livros. O objetivo do escritor era criar uma biblioteca digital que pudesse ser acessada de qualquer lugar do mundo por meio da internet, com o intuito de preservar as obras e ainda torná-las disponíveis para todas as pessoas. Hart tomou essa iniciativa quando estudava na Universidade de Illinois, nos Estados Unidos, e possuía acesso ilimitado a um computador.

Capítulo 7

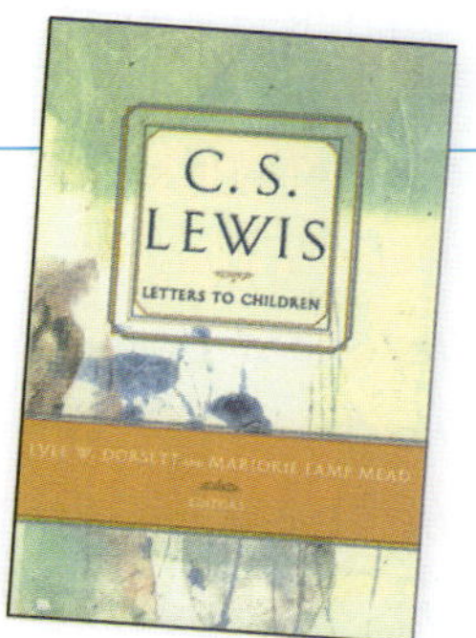

Letters to Children

Escrito por C. S. Lewis.
New York: Schribner Book Company, 1996.

Já imaginou escrever uma carta ao seu escritor favorito e receber uma resposta dele? Muitas crianças ganharam a oportunidade de ter suas perguntas respondidas por C. S. Lewis, autor irlandês da série *As crônicas de Nárnia*. Os editores Lyle W. Dorsett e Marjorie Lamp Mead transformaram essas interações em um livro, cuja primeira publicação data de 1985, composto das cartas e suas respectivas respostas. O escritor tira as dúvidas dos leitores sobre suas obras, além de aproveitar para tratar de temas como sua profissão, a escola e os animais.

Capítulo 8

Newseum

O Museu da Notícia, em Washington, D.C., Estados Unidos, conta com a tradicional coleção de artefatos e objetos antigos relacionados ao tema. No entanto, o grande atrativo do *site* oficial do museu interativo são as publicações diárias das capas de jornais de vários lugares do mundo. Por exemplo: curioso para saber como um desastre natural no Japão foi encarado pela imprensa estadunidense? Abra os *links* direcionados às capas dos jornais dos Estados Unidos e veja como muitas vezes um mesmo tema é abordado de maneiras diferentes por veículos de comunicação diversos.

Track list

Track	Unit	Activity	Page
1	Introduction	–	–
2	1	2	17
3	1	3, 4	17
4	2	2, 3	29
5	3	2	41
6	3	3	41
7	3	4, 5	41, 42
8	4	3, 4	55
9	4	5	55

Track	Unit	Activity	Page
10	5	2, 3, 4	69
11	6	2	81
12	6	3	81
13	6	4	81
14	7	2	94
15	7	3, 4	94, 95
16	7	5	95
17	8	4, 5	106, 107

References

COONTS, Stephen. ***The Art of War:* A Novel.** New York: St. Martin's Press, 2016.

GIANT, Nikki. ***E-safety for the I-generation:* Combating the Misuse and Abuse of Technology in Schools.** Philadelphia: Jessica Kingsley Publishers, 2013.

RIORDAN, Rick. ***Percy Jackson & the Olympians:* The Last Olympian.** London: Puffin, 2009.

SHELLEY, Mary W. ***Frankenstein;* or, the Modern Prometheus.** Project Gutenberg, 2008.

The Guardian, London, February 1, 2003.

The Guardian, London, February 5, 2018.

The Guardian, London, January 2, 2011.

The Jakarta Post, Mataram, December 11, 2017.

The Korea Herald, Seoul, March 28, 2018.

The Sydney Morning Herald, Sydney, December 8, 2017.

TOLKIEN, John R.R. ***The Lord of the Rings:* The Fellowship of the Ring.** London: HarperCollins Publishers, 2008.

___________. ***The Lord of the Rings:* The Return of the King.** London: HarperCollins Publishers, 2008.

WARREN, Bernie; SPITZER, Peter. ***Smiles are Everywhere:* Integrating Clown-Play into Healthcare Practice.** New York: Routledge, 2014.

What's That Stuff? Chemical & Engineering News. American Chemical Society Issue. February 26, 2018. Volume 96, Issue 9. p. 28-29.

WILSON, Jacqueline. ***Rose Rivers:* A Victorian Tale from the World of Hetty Feather.** London: Penguin Books, 2018.

YACLEY-FRANKEN, Nicki. ***Teens in Nepal.*** Minneapolis: Compass Point Books, 2008.

Zululand Observer, Empangeni, June 11, 2018.